Grade **5**

Scott Foresman

The Grammar & Writing Book

ISBN: 0-328-14639-0

6 7 8 9 10 V008 09 08 07

PEARSON

Scott
Foresman

Editorial Offices: Glenview, Illinois • Parsippany, New Jersey • New York, New York
Sales Offices: Boston, Massachusetts • Duluth, Georgia • Glenview, Illinois
Coppell, Texas • Sacramento, California • Mesa, Arizona

Table of Contents

Writer's Guide

Rubrics and Models

Evaluate Your Writing

Grammar and Writing Lessons

Writing for Tests

Grammar Patrol

Index

Writer's Guide

Focus/Ideas

Good writers **focus** on a **main idea** and develop this idea with strong, supporting details. In addition, they know their purpose for writing. This purpose may be to inform, to persuade, or to entertain. Deciding on your purpose can help you focus on your main idea and develop it effectively.

When you prepare to write, first consider possible topics. Choose the one that interests you the most. Then decide whether you want to inform, persuade, or entertain your audience. Write possible main ideas, and let your ideas flow as you plan. Don't be afraid to change your mind. Select the main idea that makes the most sense as you consider who your audience is.

List **details** that focus your topic and support your main idea. Add interesting information that will appeal to your audience. Now decide which details are the strongest.

Look at the following example. This writer has listed details and then eliminated those that do not focus on the main idea.

Main Idea   Persuade Mom to adopt a dog
Details

Will teach me responsibility   Will keep me company

Will play with me   ~~Some dogs fluffy~~

Promise to walk it every day   Will take care of it

~~I saw cute dog in park~~

Strategies for Focus and Ideas

- Choose a topic that you will enjoy writing about. If you care about your topic, you will be able to write with enthusiasm.
- If you cannot think of many supporting details, change your main idea.

A Read each writing assignment below. Write the letter of the purpose that best suits it.

    A To entertain   **B** To inform   **C** To persuade

  1. A movie review that recommends seeing the movie

  2. A tall tale about Super Chicken

  3. A report on whales

  4. A funny description of your most embarrassing moment

  5. A letter to voters telling why they should vote for you

B Read the paragraph below. Write the numbers of the sentences that do not focus on the main idea in the first sentence.

  Main idea Being a pet sitter for our neighbors has been a great job for me. **(6)** I get to give food, water, and attention to dogs and cats while their owners are away. **(7)** I love being with these animals, and they like the attention I give them. **(8)** On the other hand, I would not want to be a pet groomer. **(9)** The pets are always happy to see me, since they miss their owners and need attention. **(10)** I play with the pets, which is fun for them and for me. **(11)** One time, I thought little Babo was sick, and I did not know what to do for him. **(12)** I really enjoy the time I spend with these animals, and I even get money for it!

C Read the details about trees listed below. Write a main idea sentence about trees based on these details. Then write a paragraph using the details.

Details   roots hold soil in place
                restful and beautiful to look at
                provide shade
                provide homes for many animals
                used to make paper and wood objects of all kinds
                produce oxygen

Improving Focus/Ideas

Original

> A giraffe interests me because it looks so weird. It is giant and also looks awkward. The hippopotamus is also a weird-looking animal. But back to the giraffe. Giraffes are the tallest animals in the world. An adult stands about eighteen feet tall, and a newborn is six feet tall. The newborn grows about four feet its first year.
>
> Giraffes have strong legs and sharp hooves. They can fight off hungry lions and hyenas. Lions are fierce predators, so giraffes need all the help they can get. If necessary, giraffes can use their long legs to run away really fast.
>
> The giraffe also has a super-long neck. It can reach up into trees for food. The giraffe's favorite meal is acacia leaves. I wonder what they eat in zoos because zoos probably don't have African trees like acacias. Oh, and here's another thing. The giraffe's tongue is very long and also prehensile.

Revising Tips

Avoid a weak, general main idea statement.   Write a strong, focused statement about giraffes' traits and their usefulness.

Include only details that focus on and develop the main idea. Delete any details that do not support the main idea. (For example, delete sentences about hippopotamuses, lions, and zoos.)

Include enough details to support important points.   Each paragraph should develop the main idea by describing a trait and telling how it helps. (Add detail explaining why height is useful.)

Define terms readers probably don't know.   (Define *prehensile*.)

Write a conclusion that reinforces your main idea.   (Add an ending that ties together all your points about the main idea.)

Improved

At first glance giraffes appear gawky and awkward, but their unusual design serves them well.

The tallest animal in the world, an adult giraffe stands about eighteen feet tall. Even a newborn is six feet tall and grows four feet in its first year! This amazing height, along with excellent eyesight, makes it easy for giraffes to spot predators on the grasslands where they live.

In addition, giraffes have strong legs and sharp hooves. They can fight off hungry lions and hyenas. If necessary, giraffes can use their long legs to run away—at 35 miles an hour!

The giraffe's long neck and tongue help it reach its favorite meal— leaves from the acacia tree. The tongue, which can be 21 inches long, is prehensile. This means it can grab and hold on to objects, such as those acacia leaves the giraffe loves so much.

Next time you see a giraffe, don't think that it looks strange or funny. Instead, admire how well its parts work together!

Writer's Corner

Your main idea statement is something like a lens on a camera: through it you focus your composition. If any detail does not make the picture clearer, refocus it so that it does—or delete it.

Organization/Paragraphs

> When you write, put your ideas in an order that will help readers understand them. **Organization**—the structure, or the way ideas are put together—allows writers to show the connections among those ideas.

Here are examples of ways you can organize your writing to help readers understand the points you want to communicate:

- As a story, from beginning to middle to end
- As a comparison/contrast essay, describing likenesses and differences
- As a persuasive argument, expressing one convincing reason after another
- As a how-to report, clearly presenting a series of steps

When you begin writing, pay attention to how you organize each paragraph. The sentences in a paragraph should fit together and appear in an order that makes sense. Use words and patterns that help a reader see how ideas are related. For example, one sentence can pose a question, and the next sentence can begin to answer it.

Strategies for Organizing Ideas

- Create a graphic organizer such as a web, outline, Venn diagram, or sketch to help you organize your ideas.
- Tell events in the order in which they happened, from first to last.
- Begin a paragraph with a topic sentence that expresses the main idea, and then write details that support the main idea.
- Use order words *(first, then, after, finally)* so your writing flows smoothly.
- Use transitions *(in addition, for example, however)* to connect ideas, sentences, and paragraphs.

A Write the letter of each writing assignment with the kind of organization it calls for.

    A Story   **C** Persuasive Argument

    B Comparison/Contrast   **D** How-to Report

    1. Explain the steps in flying a kite.

    2. Tell about how you rescued your cat from a tree.

    3. Explain how a book and a movie are alike and different.

    4. Convince friends to volunteer for a charity walkathon.

B Rearrange the order of the sentences in the paragraph below so that the ideas flow smoothly. Write the new paragraph.

    (5) Then one day she went exploring, and a cat began to chase her. **(6)** She dashed into a little crack in the wall, barely beating the cat's claws. **(7)** When eating didn't work, she wished and wished on a star. **(8)** First, she tried eating lots and lots. **(9)** Once upon a time, there was a little mouse who wanted to be big. **(10)** "Thank goodness I was small enough to fit in that crack!" she said. "I guess my size is just right for me."

C Write a paragraph explaining how to choose a gift for a friend or organize a messy backpack. Use order words such as *first, then, after,* and *finally* to make ideas flow smoothly.

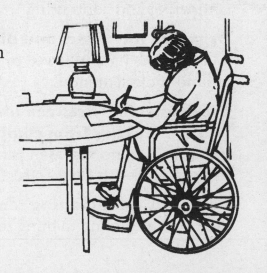

Improving Organization/Paragraphs

Original

Crayons and markers are the choices for coloring maps.

Crayons have a lot of problems, like they get dull and have to be sharpened, while markers keep a fine tip from beginning to end. Crayons and markers will put color on the map and make it more interesting to look at. Using crayons to color a big map will mean hard work and hand cramps, but so will markers.

Differences: I have to press harder with a crayon than with a marker, which releases color onto the page easily. The marker can let colors soak over the lines or even through the paper. Crayons do not "wet" the paper in that way. Crayon colors have a little bit of shine, while markers produce flatter, darker colors.

Revising Tips

Begin with a clear, focused topic sentence. Include enough information to make the subject clear. (Tell what and why you are comparing and contrasting.)

Organize likenesses and differences together logically. Discuss all likenesses first, followed by all differences. Organize information around topic sentences.

Use connectors between ideas, as well as words to signal when you are moving from comparing to contrasting. (Add *Both* and *In addition* to connect ideas in paragraphs. To move smoothly to contrasting section, start with *On the other hand...*, not *Differences:)*

End with a concluding sentence that ties ideas together. (Reword the ending to bring readers back to the main idea.)

Improved

Once again, I have a map to color, and once again, I must decide whether to use crayons or markers.

Aren't they pretty much alike, you say? Both crayons and markers will put color on the map and make it more interesting to look at. In addition, with a big map to color, using either will mean hard work and hand cramps.

On the other hand, there are some real differences between crayons and markers. While crayons get dull and have to be sharpened, markers keep that same fine tip from beginning to end. The artist also must press harder with a crayon than with a marker. The marker releases color onto paper easily, but its flow can let colors soak over the lines or even through the paper. Crayons do not "wet" the paper in that way. Crayon colors have a little bit of shine, while markers produce flatter, darker colors.

Markers or crayons . . . what do you think?

Writer's Corner

Check your organization by highlighting your topic sentence, your conclusion, and any connectors you used in the body. If they do not provide a clear path through your ideas, your readers won't be able to find their way either.

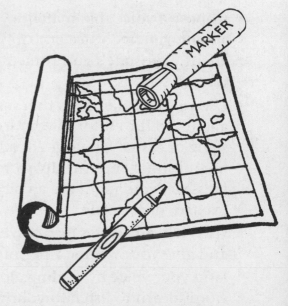

Voice

> Good writers usually have a strong **voice**—a personality that comes through in the tone and style of their writing. A strong voice speaks directly to readers and keeps their attention. Notice the difference in voice in the sentences below.
>
> - Today began nicely. I felt happy. (weak voice)
> - Today I leaped out of bed with a big smile on my face. (strong voice)

When you write, just as when you speak, you can choose the tone of voice you use. Voice helps you communicate with a certain audience for a particular purpose. The style of your writing and your choice of words can make the writing interesting to each reader, whether the tone is serious or humorous, formal or informal. If you care about your subject, your writing will reflect your voice.

Strategies for Developing Your Voice

- Choose a voice that matches your audience and purpose. For example, a light, carefree voice probably would not work for writing an essay about your state's government. Instead, you would need to use a more formal, serious tone.
- Use words and phrases that match the type of writing. For example, in a letter to the editor of your local newspaper, you should avoid using slang or casual language. In a letter to a friend, however, you would use informal and friendly words or even slang. Depending on your message, you might use a voice that is thoughtful, humorous, angry, excited, or sarcastic.
- Use vivid adjectives *(nervous, excited, calm)* to elaborate on your ideas and give your writing a personal voice.
- Find your voice by reading aloud things you have written. In other words, learn to listen to yourself.

A Match each numbered item with the type of writing it is.

> **A** Personal Narrative   **C** Persuasive Argument
>
> **B** Humorous Description   **D** Comparison/Contrast Essay

1. Join me in asking the city council for new playground equipment.
2. The Asian elephant has smaller ears than its African cousin.
3. Icing dripped off the lopsided cake, which smelled suspiciously like pepper.
4. As I coasted down the hill, I hadn't a care in the world.

B Match each kind of voice with the writing it would fit best.

> **A** Humorous   **B** Angry   **C** Friendly

5. A story about a kitten that thinks it is a fox terrier
6. An article listing ways that overly slow drivers can be a hazard on the road
7. A letter to a friend telling about an enjoyable party

C Add words or phrases to the sentences to express a strong, lively voice.

(8) I ___ fast food because ___. **(9)** My all-time ___ is ___, which taste like ___. **(10)** Whenever I eat ___, I feel ___. **(11)** If I owned a fast-food place, I would ___.

Improving Voice

Original

A mimosa tree is something I remember from visits to Grandpa's in Arkansas. They were growing in yards and in fields. Many green things dried up in the summer. The mimosas did not. They like the heat.

The tree has a straight trunk with no low branches. The branches grow higher up. They arch off to the sides. This gives the tree an unusual shape. The trees' leaves look similar to ferns. They have a surprising characteristic. When you touch them, they close up.

This genus of tree also has pink blossoms that attract butterflies and hummingbirds. Mimosas have a sweet smell. People like them as shade trees.

Revising Tips

Establish a voice in the opening paragraph. Create a voice that is appropriate to a personal memory. (Add words and expressions that convey feelings: *visions of enchanted gardens; I remember vividly*)

Use interesting language to suggest your personality and get your reader involved. Replace flat, dull sentences with vivid ones that bring the topic to life.

Elaborate on your ideas. Use precise, descriptive details rather than vague, general ones. (Replace *like the heat* with *thrive on the heat*. Replace *an unusual shape* with *a large, living umbrella*.)

Match your language to your purpose. Don't use scientific words in writing about a personal memory. (Delete *genus of tree*.)

Put yourself and your feelings into your writing. (*I could run a finger along a frond* instead of *When you touch them*)

Improved

For me, just hearing the word *mimosa* brings on visions of enchanted gardens. I remember vividly these large, welcoming trees that grow in the yards and fields around Grandpa's home in Arkansas. In the South, many green things cannot stand the wicked summer sun. However, the mimosas thrive on the heat.

The trunk stands up straight, smooth, and tall, but the branches arch off to the sides. The overall impression of a mimosa is a large, living umbrella. The trees' soft, dark green leaves are gathered in ferny-looking fronds. I could run a finger along a frond, and the leaves would close themselves up. Magic!

Then there are the hundreds of pink, puffy blossoms, as soft and fuzzy as chicks. Butterflies and hummingbirds buzz around them, drawn by their wonderful sweet smell. There is no better place to lie on a hot summer afternoon than in the shade of a mimosa tree.

Writer's Corner

Your writing voice should sound like you, which means it should sound natural and honest. Before you write, think about your subject and your connection to it. You cannot achieve a natural voice unless your topic is something you know and care about.

Word Choice

Good writers choose their **words** carefully. They use specific words to make their meaning clear. They also use vivid words to elaborate on their ideas and add excitement to their writing. Look below to see how word choice can make a sentence lively.

- Nat threw the ball to the batter. (dull)
- Nat grunted as he hurled a curve ball to the batter. (lively)

Strategies for Improving Word Choice

- Replace ordinary words with vivid words. A thesaurus, which lists synonyms, can help you. Choose words with caution though. Not all synonyms are interchangeable.
- Use exact nouns. (*hotel* instead of *place, oil painting* instead of *picture*)
- Use strong verbs. (*flinch* instead of *move, barked* instead of *said*)
- Use vivid adjectives to elaborate on your descriptions. (*tattered* instead of *old, drenched* instead of *wet*)
- Avoid vague words such as *great, nice, thing,* and *stuff.* (*I smell roses* instead of *I smell things*)
- Use strong images or figurative language to appeal to your readers' senses. (*Gillian's face turned red as a tomato* instead of *Gillian was embarrassed*)
- Decide if some sentences that have linking verbs would be stronger with action verbs. (*My heart thumped* instead of *I was excited*)
- Avoid wordiness. (*I think we will win the game because we have better players* instead of *In my opinion, I think we will win the game due to the fact that we have better players*)

A Write the more vivid or exact word to complete each sentence.

1. The little dog (walked, trotted) along the side of the road.
2. A strong breeze (sounded, rustled) in the tall grasses growing there.
3. Suddenly, the dog turned and (looked, stared) behind it.
4. It (cocked, moved) its head at a curious angle.
5. The (funny, high-pitched) noise was the whine of bicycle tires.
6. The dog's tail began to wag wildly at the sight of (someone, its owner).

B Write the letter of the word-choice strategy that correctly describes each underlined word or words.

A Exact noun   **C** Strong verb
B Vivid adjective   **D** Sense image

(7) The little <u>terrier</u> leaped up into the bike's basket. (8) It <u>settled</u> there like a lookout on a tall ship. (9) With its <u>nose lifted into the cool breeze</u>, the dog looked proud and satisfied. (10) Dog, owner, and bike traveled slowly down the <u>overgrown</u> roadway.

C Replace the underlined word or phrase in each sentence with a more exact or vivid word. Write the replacement word or phrase.

11. When they reached the <u>place</u>, they stopped.
12. The little dog <u>got</u> out of the basket.
13. Then it <u>moved</u> purposefully to the porch.
14. It stood on its <u>little</u> hind legs and scratched at the door.
15. <u>A person</u> opened the door and shuffled out.

Improving Word Choice

Original

When it is very early, Grandpa and I go to the pond with our gear. Grandpa uncovers the boat and puts the cover away. Then we get in the boat, and Grandpa puts in our stuff. The water is dark, and I can hear sounds as he moves us out to our spot. I can't see much. There is a shape on the levee.

Slowly, it gets light. Now I can see that the shape is really a bunch of blackberry bushes. We bait our hooks and cast our lines. They move through the air and land in the water. We sit in the mist and watch the sun light everything up. Lots of birds and insects make noise.

Grandpa opens the cooler. We have brought some bologna and cheese sandwiches. It is my firm opinion that the two of us, Grandpa and I, are about to have a good time.

Revising Tips

Replace vague or general nouns. Substitute the names of specific people, places, or things. (Use *rowboat* instead of *boat*; replace *stuff* with the names of items Grandpa packs.)

Use vivid verbs to describe actions precisely. (Replace *go* with *trudge*; replace *move* with *slice*; replace *is* with *stretches*.)

Elaborate with words that appeal to the senses. (*land with a soft plop in the still water* instead of *land in the water*)

Use images and figurative language to create strong word pictures. (*buzz like tiny mowing machines* to describe insect noise)

Avoid wordiness. Rewrite sentences that contain unnecessary words. (Shorten and refocus the final sentence.)

Improved

In the hour just before dawn, Grandpa and I trudge to the pond with our gear. Grandpa uncovers the rowboat and carefully folds the cover. Then we step into the boat, and Grandpa lifts in our poles, a tackle box, and the cooler. The dark water makes little splashing sounds as he rows us out to our spot. A long shadow stretches across the levee.

Slowly, light creeps in. The shadow turns out to be a thick growth of blackberry bushes. We bait our hooks silently and cast our lines. They slice through the air and land with a soft plop in the still water. We sit in the mist and watch the sun paint the day with color. A whole chorus of birds begins warbling, while insects start to buzz like tiny mowing machines.

Grandpa opens the cooler, and my mouth begins to water at the thought of bologna and cheese sandwiches. We settle in to enjoy our day.

Writer's Corner

Be on the lookout for "wow" words that make writing come alive: *silky, shiver, syrup, kerplunk, slurp, dazzle, slimy, splatter.* Keep a notebook handy to record these words.

Sentences

Good writers express their thoughts in lively, varied **sentences**. They make reading a pleasure by using sentences that create a special rhythm and style. Look at the short paragraph below. Note how the writer varies sentence type and length to make the writing interesting.

What should you keep in mind when adopting a dog? One important thing to remember is that some dogs are better than others for certain people. For example, hunting dogs need plenty of exercise. Do not get a hunting dog if you can't take her for frequent long walks. Instead, think about adopting a small dog that needs less exercise. Enjoy your new pet!

Strategies for Improving Sentences

- Write sentences that flow logically from one to the other.
- Vary sentence length by mixing short and long sentences.
- Avoid sentences that are too long or wordy. You might rewrite a very long sentence as two or more shorter sentences.
- Avoid writing a series of short, choppy sentences. Use connectors such as *and, but, or, because, although,* and *until* to join two simple, related sentences.
- Include different kinds of sentences to add variety and life to your writing. Although most sentences will be statements, include some questions, commands, and exclamations too.
- Vary the beginnings of sentences. Avoid starting every sentence with words such as *I, she, he, then,* or *the.*
- Read what you write aloud to yourself. Listen for a rhythm as if you are listening to a song. Rewrite sentences that interrupt the flow.

A Combine these short, choppy sentences. Use the connector in ( ) where the blank is. Add a comma if necessary. Write the sentence.

1. I like going to the city. ___ There is so much to do. (because)

2. Sometimes we drive in. ___ Usually we take the train. (but)

3. Mom's favorite place is the art museum. ___ Mine is the science museum. (and)

4. ___ We sit in a park to rest our feet. We watch boats in the harbor. (while)

5. ___ We are very tired at the end of the day. We love these outings. (although)

B Each sentence in the following paragraph is too long. Rewrite each one as two or more sentences. Remember to add capital letters and correct end punctuation.

(6) My cousin June lives in the city and she likes to visit our farm and comes every summer for two weeks. **(7)** It is fun for me because June is funny and we like the same things, for example, we both like riding bikes and playing video games. **(8)** It is also fun to have June stay in my room because we tell jokes and stories after we go to bed and sometimes we read stories to each other. **(9)** This summer I will be raising a heifer for the competition at the country fair and June will love helping me feed and care for it. **(10)** June is just like a sister to me and I can't wait for her to come and spend time with our family this year.

C Write a paragraph that describes a place you especially like to visit. Include at least one command and one question. Include both long and short sentences.

Improving Sentences

Original

I have a new motto. I will give new places a chance. I visited South Dakota. I didn't want to go. I thought it sounded boring.

I was in for quite a surprise. We went to Mount Rushmore last. Our first stop in South Dakota was in Mitchell. We visited the Corn Palace. It has onion domes and towers on top. It looks like something out of Aladdin. The walls have murals. The murals are made from corn and other grain.

We rolled on to the Badlands National Park and it is mountains carved into wild shapes by wind and water and it has rainbow colors. Then we went to Custer State Park. It has a big buffalo herd. Buffalo cross the road and stop cars. At Mount Rushmore, four presidents gaze at you. Their faces are carved in the stone. South Dakota is one of my favorite places.

Revising Tips

Vary sentence openings.   Avoid starting too many sentences with *I*. (Rewrite some sentences in the first paragraph.)

Join short, choppy sentences.   Connectors such as *and, but, although, where,* and *because* show how ideas are related.

Avoid sentences that are too long or wordy.   (Create several sentences from the first sentence of the last paragraph.)

Order sentences for a logical flow.   (Remove *We went to Mount Rushmore last* and put this information at the end of the essay.)

Vary kinds and lengths of sentences.   Rephrase some statements as exclamations, questions, or commands.

Improved

Always give new places a chance. This is what I learned on my trip to South Dakota. Before we went, I complained constantly, "It sounds boring. Can't I stay home?"

What a surprise I was in for! Our first stop in South Dakota was in Mitchell, where we visited the Corn Palace. It has onion domes and towers on top and looks like something out of Aladdin. The walls are covered with murals made from corn and other grains.

We then rolled on to the Badlands National Park. There, wind and water have carved mountains into wild shapes in rainbow colors. In Custer State Park, a big buffalo herd caused a traffic jam. Finally, we arrived at Mount Rushmore, where the stone faces of Washington, Jefferson, Lincoln, and Theodore Roosevelt gazed down at us. Since this trip, South Dakota has become one of my favorite places.

Writer's Corner

Well-constructed sentences should flow smoothly into one another. To make sure yours do, read your finished paper aloud. Any sentences you trip over will probably trip up your audience too.

Conventions

A **convention** is a rule that people agree to follow. Written language follows special conventions. For example, sentences begin with capital letters and end with some kind of punctuation. Sentences about the same topic are grouped together to form paragraphs. Conventions also set rules for spelling and grammar. How many conventions can you name in the sentences below?

- Greg Harding was born in Nashville, Tennessee, on March 3, 1996.
- He is a student at Griffin Elementary School, and his favorite classes are English and math.

Strategies for Conventions

- Learn the rules for spelling. For example, add *-s* or *-es* to form the plural of most nouns.
- Use a dictionary or spell checker to help you with the spelling of difficult or new words.
- Capitalize the first word in a sentence and each important word in proper nouns.
- Use punctuation correctly.
- Make sure each verb you use agrees with its subject.
- Check that the verb tenses are correct.
- Check that pronouns in subjects and predicates are correct.
- Do not run sentences together without proper punctuation.
- Use Proofreading Marks as you revise and edit your work.

Proofreading Marks

⁋	New paragraph
≡	Capital letter
/	Lowercase letter
◯	Correct the spelling.
∧	Add something.
ℒ	Remove something.

A Write the correct word in ( ) to complete each sentence.

1. (grandma, Grandma) is finding out about our family history.
2. She uses (her, hers) computer to get information.
3. Some of our ancestors (was, were) from England.
4. Some of (them, they) were from Germany.
5. I think (its, it's) interesting to learn family history, (don't, doesn't) you?

B Match the letter with the mistake in each sentence.

A Correct a misspelling.
B Capitalize a proper noun.
C Add correct end punctuation.
D Make the verb agree with its subject.
E Add an apostrophe.

(6) My favorite uncles name is Wilbur. **(7)** Wilbur lives in scottsdale, Arizona, but he travels all over the world. **(8)** He has the most fantastic collection of postcards of anyone **(9)** Whenever I visit Uncle Wilbur, I spends hours looking at postcards of wonderful places. **(10)** Uncle Wilbur promised to take me on a trip for my aith grade graduation.

C Write five sentences about one of the topics below. Make sure you follow the conventions for proper spelling, grammar, punctuation, and capitalization.

- Your town or state
- Your family history
- Your favorite relative

MY FAMILY TREE

Improving Conventions

Original

Every family has a character that stands out from the rest for me, that character is Aunt Fiona. It isn't her curly red hair and freckles because my brother and me have those too. Aunt Fiona talks enthusiastically with everyone she meets, but Dad says thats just "the McNulty talking gene."

These traits is special, but what makes Aunt Fiona extra wonderful is her spirit of adventure. She love to travel and has gone all over the world. She taught english to japanese children so she could visit Asia. Before that, she worked as a messenger, she took important papers all over for big companys. In a month, she might go to France, Italy, and Australia. Her first job was the peace corps. Aunt Fiona spent two years in Africa, helping build schooles for children.

To Aunt Fiona, the most important goal is to satisfy you're curiosity about the world. She makes me want to have exciting adventures around the world too.

Revising Tips

Do not run sentences together incorrectly. (For example, add a period after *rest* and capitalize *for* in the first paragraph.)

Make sure that subjects and verbs agree. (*These traits are special* instead of *These traits is special; She loves* instead of *She love*)

Use an apostrophe in contractions. (*that's* instead of *thats*)

Use the correct pronoun form. (*my brother and I* instead of *my brother and me; your* instead of *you're*)

Capitalize all proper nouns and adjectives. (*English* and *Japanese* instead of *english* and *japanese; Peace Corps* instead of *peace corps*)

Form plurals of nouns correctly. (Correct *schooles* and *companys*.)

Improved

Every family has a character that stands out from the rest. For me, that character is Aunt Fiona. It isn't her curly red hair and freckles because my brother and I have those too. Aunt Fiona talks enthusiastically with everyone she meets, but Dad says that's just "the McNulty talking gene."

These traits are special, but what makes Aunt Fiona extra wonderful is her spirit of adventure. She loves to travel and has gone all over the world. She taught English to Japanese children so she could visit Asia. Before that, she worked as a messenger. She took important papers all over for big companies. In a month, she might go to France, Italy, and Australia. Her first job was in the Peace Corps. Aunt Fiona spent two years in Africa, helping build schools for children.

To Aunt Fiona, the most important goal is to satisfy your curiosity about the world. She makes me want to have exciting adventures around the world too.

Writer's Craft

You can catch many errors by proofreading your work with "fresh eyes." Put your finished paper aside for a while; then reread it. That time away from your paper will make errors stand out.

Rubrics and Models

Narrative Writing *Scoring Rubric*

A scoring **rubric** can be used to judge a piece of writing. A rubric is a checklist of traits, or writing skills, to look for. See pages 2–25 for a discussion of these traits. Rubrics give a number score for each trait.

Score	4	3	2	1
Focus/Ideas	Excellent narrative focused on a clear main idea; much elaboration	Good narrative mostly focused on a main idea; some elaboration	Unfocused narrative with unrelated details	Rambling narrative with unrelated details
Organization/ Paragraphs	Strong beginning, middle, and end, with appropriate order words	Adequate beginning, middle, and end, with some order words	Little direction from beginning to end, with few order words	Lacks beginning, middle, end; incorrect or no order words
Voice	Writer involved— personality evident	Reveals personality at times	Little writer involvement, personality	Careless writing with no feeling
Word Choice	Vivid, precise words that bring the story to life	Adequate words to bring the story to life	Few vivid or interesting words	Vague, dull, or misused words
Sentences	Excellent variety of sentences; natural rhythm	Varied lengths, styles; generally smooth	Simple, awkward, or wordy sentences; little variety	Choppy; many incomplete or run-on sentences
Conventions	Excellent control; few or no errors	No serious errors to affect understanding	Weak control; enough errors to affect understanding	Many errors that prevent understanding

Following are four models that respond to a prompt. Each model has been given a score, based on the rubric.

Writing Prompt   Write about an exciting or unforgettable event in your life. Be sure your narrative has a beginning, middle, and end. Use vivid words to help readers see and feel what you experienced.

Narrative Writing Model *Score 4*

Three years ago, my life changed completely. That's when my little sister Allie was born. When I first went to the hospital to see her, she was tiny and cute and screamed louder than all the other babies. That should have given me a clue. Allie wanted attention, now!

At first, Allie slept all the time—during the day. She did that so she could cry at night. Mom was so sleepy some mornings she would give me cereal without a bowl! Luckily, Allie soon learned how to smile and coo. She learned really fast that smiling could get her anything she wanted—crackers, apple juice, toys. We became pals right away.

Now Allie is three and follows me all over. I teach her new things, like salsa steps and songs. Allie still loves attention, and I love giving it to her.

Focus/Ideas Details support main idea that Allie loves attention.

Organization/Paragraphs Events in order; connectors between paragraphs make passage of time clear *(three years ago, at first, now)*

Voice Writer's personality evident through details, style *(my life changed completely, I love giving it to her)*

Word Choice Exact nouns *(hospital, salsa)*, strong verbs *(screamed, coo)*, vivid adjectives *(tiny, sleepy)*

Sentences Lively, varied sentences with distinct rhythm

Conventions No errors

Narrative Writing Model *Score 3*

My tenth birthday was last sumer and I will never forget that day!
My party had to be put off because Wes got chicken pox. That morning
when I woke up, it was raining. So I said This is the worst birthday ever.

Dad told me to sweep the garage. By then I was really feeling sorry for
myself. There was a note taped to the door. It said look in the big box in
the corner. Inside was a sleeping puppy!

That's how I got Iggles, my best friend and my very own dog. Iggles
is a beagle. He is still a puppy but about half growd. We run and play
together every day.

Focus/Ideas   Details mostly support main idea of unforgettable
birthday

Organization/Paragraphs   Events mostly in order; some connecting
words to help flow of paragraphs *(that morning, by then)*

Voice   Writer's feelings clear *(will never forget; worst birthday)*

Word Choice   Some words too general *(big box, got);* be verbs overused

Sentences   Clear sentences; some variety

Conventions   Some errors in punctuation
(compound sentence, direct quotations);
a spelling error *(sumer)* and a usage error *(growd)*

Narrative Writing Model *Score 2*

One time I clim a tree. Its a tree in my yard and its really big and scary and Ryan dared me to clim it. So I said no so he said I was chiken. I started up the tree. It is a pine tree. The bark is scratchy and sticky. Ryan is my neighbor and he is a year older than me. Sometimes we have fun sometimes he makes me mad. His house is a lot bigger than ours too. I got up pretty far on the tree then I got scared. So I started down but I slipped and lost my balence. I fell to the ground. My arm hurt bad. It was in a cast for six weeks. That was bad cuz it itched.

Focus/Ideas   Focused on event; some unrelated details *(His house is a lot bigger . . .)*; not enough elaboration to bring event to life

Organization/Paragraphs   Events mostly in order; some sentences misplaced *(Ryan is . . . . makes me mad)*

Voice   Some feelings expressed *(I got scared)*

Word Choice   A few vivid words *(bark is scratchy and sticky)*; many general, dull words *(big, fun, mad, got)*

Sentences   Poor flow, rhythm; little variety

Conventions   Misspellings *(clim, Its, chiken, balence, cuz)*; grammatical errors *(bad* instead of *badly, older than me)*; run-on sentences

Narrative Writing Model *Score 1*

Buddy and me went to the state far. Jodie taked us it was big. I liked the farus weel and the animals too and we went in jodies truck it is red. So we saw the cows and sheep and pigs and rabbits and that was fun. The tractor pull was most fun. You can get elefant ears that is hot and good we got lemenad Buddy falled asleep on the way home and it was a good day.

Focus/Ideas   No main idea to focus paper

Organization/Paragraphs   Events out of order; no paragraphs

Voice   Conveys writer's personality

Word Choice   Limited, dull word choice *(went, fun, got, was)*

Sentences   Long, stringy sentences; overuse of *and*

Conventions   Errors in punctuation, capitalization, spelling *(far, farus weel, elefant, lemenad)*, verb usage *(taked, falled)*, pronoun, and apostrophe *(jodies)*; run-on sentences

Descriptive Writing *Scoring Rubric*

Score	4	3	2	1
Focus/Ideas	Excellent description with clear main idea and strong, elaborated details	Good description with adequate details focused on main idea	Some descriptive details; some focus on main idea	Little focus on described subject; lacks details
Organization/ Paragraphs	Details arranged in a clear order; strong beginning and ending	Details mostly arranged in order; good beginning and ending	Details not well connected; weak beginning or ending	No organization to details; lack of beginning or ending
Voice	Strong personality; clear connection between writer and subject	Writer involved; some connection between writer and subject	Writer lacking involvement; few feelings shown	Writer involvement, point of view missing
Word Choice	Specific, vivid language that appeals to several senses	Accurate, engaging language that appeals to one or two senses	Uninteresting language; little appeal to senses	Limited, vague language; repetitive
Sentences	Superior structure; excellent flow	Some varied beginnings; well constructed	Simple structures; little variety	Many errors; awkward; hard to read
Conventions	Excellent control; few or no errors	No serious errors to affect understanding	Weak control; enough errors to affect understanding	Many errors that prevent understanding

Following are four models that respond to a prompt. Each model has been given a score, based on the rubric.

Writing Prompt Write a description of a place or a living thing in nature. Use exact words to help readers see, hear, taste, smell, and feel what you are describing.

Descriptive Writing Model *Score 4*

The lagoon in our town is a wonderful recreation place. Bigger than a pond but smaller than a lake, the lagoon is just right for summer or winter fun.

In summer, children feed the geese that swim there. Babies squeal with delight as the white birds paddle eagerly after chunks of bread. The banks under the big old trees provide a quiet spot for fishing. Sometimes I sit on the twisted tree roots and watch canoers paddling by.

In winter, kids of all ages put on their skates and glide over the ice. On the banks, someone makes a fragrant cedar fire in the stone pit, and shivering skaters crowd around. In late afternoon, as the sun sets, the ice and the snow-covered trees take on a pink glow.

Our town is lucky. Our lagoon provides an escape to nature in any season.

Focus/Ideas   Specific details that bring the lagoon into focus

Organization/Paragraphs   Organized by seasons with clear connecting words between paragraphs; strong beginning and ending

Voice   Clear communication of enjoyment; enthusiasm for place

Word Choice   Vivid verbs and modifiers that appeal to sight (*paddle, twisted, glide, snow-covered, pink*) hearing (*squeal*), smell (*fragrant cedar fire*), and feeling (*shivering*)

Sentences   Interest through variation in sentence type and length

Conventions   No mechanical errors

Descriptive Writing Model *Score 3*

> I was sitting outside in the yard when I saw it. It flew so fast it was a blur. All I saw was this bright green. Culd a bug really be that color? Then all a sudden I saw it clearly. It was hovering like a helicopter. By the bird bath. Like a helicopter it moved forward and backward very quickly.
>
> I could not believe it. Now it was on a flower stem next to me! I could see it had two wings on each side. Their surface looked like window screens. The body was like a long, skinny stick. The head was that bright green color like I said. I tried to sneak even closer, but it took off it could really move fast!
>
> Later, I found out that this strange insect was a dragonfly.

Focus/Ideas   All details focused on the subject of the mysterious insect

Organization/Paragraphs   Details in logical order with good connecting words; build up to ending where insect is identified

Voice   Writer's excitement communicated

Word Choice   A few strong verbs and modifiers that appeal to sight *(hovering, like window screens);* some unnecessary repetition *(bright green)*

Sentences   Mostly complete sentences; some variety in type and length

Conventions   A spelling error *(Culd)*, a run-on sentence, and a fragment

Descriptive Writing Model *Score 2*

I was at Grandmas and a chipmunk suprize me. We were sitting outside.
Be quite now Grandma said. Then this little fury animal ran up the sidewalk.
He looks like a little squirrel with stripes on his back except his tail was
straight not curled. He ran fast. He has dark and light stripes on his back.
Grandma said we should leave him our bread crusts. The next morning they
are gone. I put food there every day. I got to see him eat. He gets a piece
of apple. He sat up and ate it. Thats it.

Focus/Ideas   Focused on the subject; some descriptive details

Organization/Paragraphs   Most details in order; needs more
connecting words; weak beginning and end; no paragraphs

Voice   Writer's personality shown

Word Choice   A few sight details; some descriptive words

Sentences   Mostly short; many beginning with *He*

Conventions   Errors in spelling (*suprize, quite* instead of *quiet, fury*),
punctuation, verb tense, and apostrophe use *(Thats)*

Descriptive Writing Model *Score 1*

One time me and my Mom went to the grand canyen. We had a flat tire and it was hot we finely got there. It was very big and it was made from a river cutting in the rocks. I showt but theres no ekko. You can see far down then we went down and we rode on buros that was fun. the rock was orange and brown. I like buros there ears are funny.

Focus/Ideas   Starts with Grand Canyon but loses focus with details on burros

Organization/Paragraphs   No connecting words between ideas; no paragraphs; no ending

Voice   Writer's feeling for subject clear

Word Choice   Mostly general words; few modifiers; details appealing to sound and sight

Sentences   Too many sentences connected with *and* and *then*

Conventions   Errors in spelling *(canyen, ekko, buros, there* instead of *their, showt)*, capitalization, pronoun and verb use; incorrect use of apostrophe *(theres)*; run-ons

Persuasive Writing *Scoring Rubric*

Score	4	3	2	1
Focus/Ideas	Excellent persuasive essay with clearly stated opinion and strong elaboration	Clear opinion supported by mostly persuasive reasons	Opinion not clearly stated; weak reasons or not enough reasons to support it	No stated opinion; details not focused on topic
Organization/ Paragraphs	Strong, convincing introduction; reasons presented in order of importance	Interesting introduction; reasons in order of importance	Weak or unclear introduction; reasons not clear or not in order of importance	No introduction; few reasons; order not logical
Voice	Concerned, committed writer behind words	Some sense of caring, concerned writer behind words	Little sense of writer involvement with essay	No sense of writer's personality or feelings evident
Word Choice	Effective use of persuasive words	Use of persuasive words adequate to good	Few persuasive words used in essay	No persuasive words used in essay
Sentences	Varied sentence structures; excellent flow and rhythm	Some varied sentence structures; few sentence errors	Limited to simple sentence structures; some errors	Simple, choppy sentences; fragments and run-ons
Conventions	Excellent control of all mechanical aspects of writing	Few errors in grammar, spelling, punctuation, paragraphing	Some distracting mechanical errors	Many errors that prevent understanding

Following are four models that respond to a prompt. Each model has been given a score, based on the rubric.

Writing Prompt   What is one way schools can help students learn better? Present your opinion and persuade your readers to accept it by giving several strong reasons in support of it.

Persuasive Writing Model *Score 4*

Mountain climbing would provide a fun, healthful, and educational opportunity for our class. It doesn't have to be Mt. Everest. Let's be realistic! We can climb a mountain in Vermont.

A mountain-climbing trip would be like an extended field trip! It would be fun to travel, meet new people, and take a break from the classroom routine.

Mountain climbing also provides excellent health benefits. We would get a great physical workout. Even better, our minds would be challenged as we follow directions, stay alert, and pull ourselves up rocky paths. Reaching the summit would give us a great feeling of accomplishment.

Best of all, mountain climbing is a learning experience that requires teamwork. Without communication and cooperation, someone could get lost or injured. This teamwork would carry over to the classroom.

I hope you will agree that this trip would be a terrific boost to improve our performance at school.

Focus/Ideas   Argument focused on clear main idea; good support

Organization/Paragraphs   Topic sentences within essay give reasons in order; most important one signaled with *Best of all*

Voice   Writer involved with topic and knowledgeable about it

Word Choice   Persuasive words with emotional appeal *(healthful, educational, excellent, benefits, terrific boost)*

Sentences   Various lengths and structures; smooth connectors *(Even better)*

Conventions   No mechanical errors

Persuasive Writing Model *Score 3*

Students should learn by doing, not just read books and listen to teachers. Would you rather read about painting a picture, or paint a picture? Plenty of students get bored with school because they just read books and listen to teachers talk.

In scouts, we made birdhouses. Now I know exactly what to use and how to make a birdhouse. If I just read about it, I couldn't do it. Doing things helps you understand what you read.

Students could learn many useful things in school. Things that go beyond books. One time we studied food groups. We could have shopped for food and cooked it. Then we will know a lot more about foods. We could even make food to sell. For example, if we made bread, we could sell it. Then we learn about busness too.

Students learn more by doing!

Focus/Ideas   Clear opinion and good examples

Organization/Paragraphs   Few connectors to show why one reason is more important

Voice   Feelings about topic clearly communicated

Word Choice   Some persuasive words and phrases *(should, helps you understand)*

Sentences   Some sentence variety

Conventions   Error in spelling *(busness)*; verb tense *(will* instead of *would)*; one sentence fragment

Persuasive Writing Model *Score 2*

I don't like social studies. The book is too hard and its boring. I would like it better if I got to choose my own topics and books to read.

Kids know what they like. If they get to pick things that interest them, I don't mind reading and doing stuff. Sometimes I don't pay attenshun in class. because the subject is boring. Last year Mr. Ito had us choose a project. To read a book about the American revolution or make a time line. That was fun. I read a story about Johnny Tremain. He was an apprentice for Paul Revere. A kid's view of the war.

Focus/Ideas   Opinion is presented, but unimportant details weaken writer's argument *(Johnny Tremain . . . apprentice for Paul Revere)*

Organization/Paragraphs   Reasons for opinion somewhat hard to follow; no conclusion

Voice   Feelings about topic communicated

Word Choice   Few persuasive words; words often general or vague *(stuff, boring, fun)*

Sentences   No smooth flow between sentences

Conventions   Errors in spelling *(attenshun)*, apostrophe use *(its* instead of *it's)*, capitalization, and pronoun use; several fragments

Persuasive Writing Model *Score 1*

Give us a reward for stuff. Such as they could get a fun toy for homework. Or a candy bar for a test. You do all this work then you have to take a test. What fun is that. We had a pizza party and we read a hundred books and everybody likes presents like I get a game if I do all my chores for a munth I didnt think it would work but nobody nags me I just do it. A really big reward, like everybody passed in the grading period, then the teacher could take the class on a feld trip.

Focus/Ideas   No clearly stated opinion or reasons

Organization/Paragraphs   No paragraphing or introduction; a jumble of sentences

Voice Identifiable voice

Word Choice   Vague, general words *(stuff, get, do, take, had, big)*; no persuasive words

Sentences   Overuse of *and* and *then* as connectors; ideas poorly or incompletely communicated

Conventions   Errors in spelling *(munth, feld),* end punctuation, pronoun agreement, and apostrophe use *(didnt* instead of *didn't)*; many fragments and run-ons

Expository Writing *Scoring Rubric*

Score	4	3	2	1
Focus/Ideas	Excellent explanation; main idea developed with strong details	Good explanation of main idea; details that mostly support it	Some focus on main idea; few supporting details	Main idea unfocused or lacking; few supporting details
Organization/ Paragraphs	Main idea in clear topic sentence; details in order; appropriate connecting words	Adequate topic sentence; most details in correct order; some connecting words	Topic sentence, important details missing or in wrong order; few connecting words	No clear order to details or connecting words to show relationships; no clear topic sentence
Voice	Engaging, but serious and rather formal	Mostly serious, but may have inappropriate shifts	Voice not always appropriate to subject matter	Voice lacking or inappropriate
Word Choice	Topic conveyed through specific, vivid language	Topic portrayed with clear language	Some vague, repetitive, or incorrect words	Dull language; very limited word choices
Sentences	Well-crafted, varied sentences	Accurate sentence construction; some variety	Little variety; overly simple constructions; some errors	Many fragments, run-ons; sense hard to follow
Conventions	Excellent control of all mechanical aspects of writing	Few mechanical errors	Some distracting mechanical errors	Many errors in mechanics that prevent understanding

Following are four models that respond to a prompt. Each model has been given a score, based on the rubric.

Writing Prompt   Write an expository paragraph explaining how a process in nature works. For example, you could write about the seasons or the stages in the life of a plant or animal. Do research if necessary to gather facts and supporting details.

Expository Writing Model *Score 4*

All plants go through a cycle in which they grow and reproduce. The cycle starts when insects such as bees carry pollen into the flower of a grown plant. They pollinate the flower so the plant can reproduce, and at this point a fruit begins to form. This fruit can be anything that contains seeds, such as a nut or berry. Each seed contains a baby plant called an embryo. The seed gets buried in the ground—it falls by itself or someone plants it. Then the embryo starts to grow. Soon the tiny plant puts out roots into the soil and a stem and leaves above the ground. Now we begin to see the plant we recognize. It will make its own flowers and begin the growing cycle again. In many flowers and vegetable plants, this whole cycle occurs in one year.

Focus/Ideas   Clear main idea; all detail sentences develop it

Organization/Paragraphs   Strong topic sentence; cycle steps presented in proper order; connectors help sense *(when, at this point, soon)*

Voice   Natural and friendly but does not intrude into explanation

Word Choice   Precise, accurate words to explain process *(pollinate, embryo, cycle)*

Sentences   Good variety; excellent flow of ideas

Conventions   Excellent control; no mechanical errors

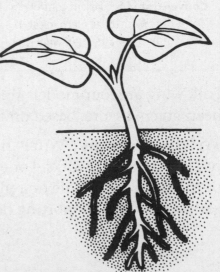

Expository Writing Model *Score 3*

A frog looks very different in the different stages of its life. It starts out as an egg layed by a female frog in a pond. A male frog swims along and fertilizes the egg. The fertilized egg hatches into a tadpole. It don't look like a frog at all but a fat, wiggly minnow. I have seen tadpoles, and boy, you'd never think they were going to be frogs! The tadpole lives in the water. It swims, breathes with gills, and grows. It grows back legs. Then it grows front legs. The tail starts to disappear. All this time, the tadpole is getting bigger. The young frog develops lungs. Now it can leave the water and breth air. It is an adult frog.

Focus/Ideas   Main idea clear, with most details focused on frog life cycle

Organization/Paragraphs   Topic sentence followed by stages in order; could use more connecting words

Voice   Mostly serious tone; writer's personality distracts at one point *(I have seen tadpoles, and boy, . . .)*

Word Choice   Some specific, vivid words *(fat, wiggly, minnow, tadpole, gills)*

Sentences   Some short, choppy sentences; natural flow lacking

Conventions   Few mechanical errors; spelling errors *(layed, breth)* and error in subject-verb agreement *(It don't)*

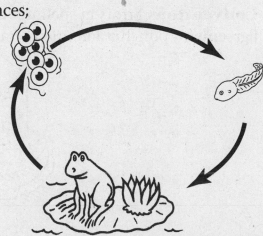

Expository Writing Model *Score 2*

How does food get turned into energy in your body? Digestion is how. Foods contain things. Like water, protein, carbodrates, and fats. Other things in food is vitamens and minerals. Digestion breaks down the food. Your stomach has chemicals that break it down. It looks gross then. It goes into the intestines. How does your body use all this stuff? For example, protein gets through the intestine wall into the blood. Or a carbodrate. Sugar is one carbodrate you need it for energy. The protein is for building new cells or fixing broken ones. Oh, and your mouth is where digestion begins.

Focus/Ideas Main idea presented; some irrelevant details included

Organization/Paragraphs Uses question as a topic sentence; some material out of order; lack of clear connecting words; lacks conclusion

Voice Often does not match serious subject matter (*It looks gross then*)

Word Choice Most words too general (*get, has, goes, stuff*)

Sentences Simple, choppy sentences

Conventions Errors in spelling (*carbodrates, vitamens*), subject-verb agreement, punctuation; many fragments; a run-on

Expository Writing Model *Score 1*

> We have four sezons. winter, spring, summer, and fall. I like summer best. Why is it cold in winter I found out in north America, the sunlite hits us different. It is not so warm. So we has snow and ice the sun hits earth different at different times. Because it is not straight up and down. Then in summer it is hot. Sunlite hits us straight, like if a lamp was moved close so it feels hot. In summer I like to go swimming. In winter I sledding.

Focus/Ideas   Several unimportant details; strays from focus

Organization/Paragraphs   No clear topic sentence; details do not explain process fully; lack of connectors for flow

Voice   No clear voice

Word Choice   Vocabulary inadequate for concept *(hits, different, straight)*, awkward; attempts a comparison to illustrate

Sentences   Little variety

Conventions   Errors in spelling *(sezons, sunlite)*, capitalization, punctuation, adverb form, pronoun-verb agreement, and verb forms; run-on and fragment errors

Evaluate Your Writing

You can evaluate your own writing by reading it over carefully. Think about what is good as well as what you can improve. As you read, ask yourself the following questions.

How does my writing sound? Read it aloud to find out.

- If it sounds choppy, you might combine short sentences.
- Are there many sentences strung together with *and, because,* or *then?* "Unhook" a long stringy sentence by separating it into several sentences.
- Do most sentences begin with *I, the, it, she,* or *he?* Think of other ways to begin these sentences. Simply rearranging words might do the trick.
- Do ideas seem connected? If not, add transition words or phrases such as *finally* or *on the other hand.* These words connect ideas and help your sentences flow.

Is the style appropriate? Who is your audience? (friends, your principal, a newspaper editor) What is your purpose? (to inform, to persuade, to entertain) Sentence fragments, informal language, and slang may be appropriate for e-mails or quick notes among friends. A more formal style suits written assignments.

Does your writing address the assignment?

- Look for key words in the writing prompt. For example:

    Compare and contrast a bike and a car.
    Tell two similarities and two differences.

    Topic: bike and car

    What you need to do: Compare and contrast

    What to include: Two similarities and two differences

- Other kinds of key words in writing prompts include *describe, explain, summarize, examples, why,* and *how.*

Is your writing focused?   Are all the sentences about the main idea? Take out or refocus sentences that wander off into unimportant details.

Is there enough elaboration and support?   Your writing may be unclear if you don't elaborate on your ideas. Supply information that readers need to know.

- Use sensory details to make your writing seem fresh and to give readers pictures, but avoid sounding flowery.
- If you give an opinion, supply strong supporting reasons.
- Expand on a main idea with several telling details.
- When necessary, define a term or give examples.

Is your beginning strong?   Does a question, a surprising fact, or an amusing detail capture a reader's interest?

Is your ending satisfying?   A conclusion may restate the main idea in a new way, tell what you feel or what you have learned, or pose a question to readers to think about. Whatever it does, it should signal that you have finished.

Have you used effective words—and not too many of them?   Have you chosen your words carefully?

- Strong verbs, precise nouns, and vivid adjectives make your writing clear and lively.
- Are there awkward phrases you can replace with a word or two? For example, replace *due to the fact that* with *because* and *at this point in time* with *now*.

Check List

- [ ] My writing sounds smooth and easy to read.

- [ ] I have used an appropriate style for my audience and purpose.

- [ ] My writing addresses the prompt or assignment.

- [ ] My writing is focused.

- [ ] I have used enough elaboration and support.

- [ ] I have a strong beginning.

- [ ] I have a satisfying conclusion.

- [ ] I have used effective words and avoided wordiness.

Grammar and
Writing Lessons

Four Kinds of Sentences

Each kind of sentence begins with a capital letter and has a special end mark.

- A **declarative sentence** makes a statement. It ends with a period.

   A good vocabulary makes you a better reader.

- An **interrogative sentence** asks a question. It ends with a question mark.

   Do you know what the word *loquacious* means?

- An **imperative sentence** gives a command or makes a request. It ends with a period. The subject (*you*) does not appear, but it is understood.

   Learn these fifty words by Friday.

- An **exclamatory sentence** shows strong feeling. It ends with an exclamation mark.

   You have got to be kidding! What a hard test that was!

- An **interjection** is a word or a group of words that expresses strong feeling. It is not a complete sentence.

   Wow! My goodness! Hooray! Ouch!

A Write *D* if the sentence is declarative. Write *IN* if the sentence is interrogative. Write *IM* if the sentence is imperative. Write *E* if the sentence is exclamatory.

1. Is it hard for you to spell words?
2. I really enjoy a game called Scrabble®.
3. Pick up seven of the letter tiles.
4. Players spell words with their letters.
5. What a terrible bunch of letters I have!

B Write each sentence, adding capitalization and the correct end mark. Then write *D* if the sentence is declarative, *IM* if it is imperative, *IN* if it is interrogative, or *E* if it is exclamatory.

1. how can I build my vocabulary

2. look in this thesaurus

3. a thesaurus lists synonyms for words

4. wow! What a lot of synonyms there are for *big*

5. how do you remember new words

6. i try to use the new word often each day

7. please write original sentences with your vocabulary words

8. what are synonyms and antonyms

9. synonyms have similar meanings

10. think of a synonym for *happy*

C Complete each sentence with words from the box. Write the sentences using capitalization and correct end marks.

to look at the examples	is a useful tool
a lot of definitions	are listed for the word *set*
does it contain	this dictionary is

11. the dictionary ____

12. what information ____

13. how many meanings ____

14. wow, that's ____

15. don't forget ____

16. what a heavy book ____

Test Preparation

✓ Read the paragraph. Write the letter of the word that identifies each kind of sentence.

(1) I need to buy a dictionary. (2) Look in the Reference Books section of the bookstore. (3) Which dictionary is best for a fifth-grade student? (4) What an amazing variety there is! (5) Buy that small one if you just need basic information. (6) Do you need a dictionary that lists word histories? (7) Get the one with 225,000 entries. (8) It is heavy but will serve you for years. (9) What is that enormous dictionary? (10) It contains every word and its history.

1. A declarative
   B interrogative
   C imperative
   D exclamatory

2. A declarative
   B interrogative
   C imperative
   D exclamatory

3. A declarative
   B interrogative
   C imperative
   D exclamatory

4. A declarative
   B interrogative
   C imperative
   D exclamatory

5. A declarative
   B interrogative
   C imperative
   D exclamatory

6. A declarative
   B interrogative
   C imperative
   D exclamatory

7. A declarative
   B interrogative
   C imperative
   D exclamatory

8. A declarative
   B interrogative
   C imperative
   D exclamatory

9. A declarative
   B interrogative
   C imperative
   D exclamatory

10. A declarative
    B interrogative
    C imperative
    D exclamatory

Review

 Write the mark that should end each sentence. Then write *D* if the sentence is declarative, *IN* if it is interrogative, *IM* if it is imperative, and *E* if it is exclamatory.

1. I am attending a new school this year
2. At first, it was quite a challenge
3. Was it easy to make new friends
4. Remember to smile at people
5. Ask them about their interests
6. How did you learn your way around
7. My lockermate was a big help
8. How relieved you must have been
9. The teachers were very nice too
10. Now I feel quite at home here

 Write each sentence. Make any necessary corrections in capitalization and punctuation.

11. in fifth grade, we have a team of teachers
12. who is on your team
13. what subject do you have first
14. language arts is my favorite subject
15. please read this book
16. wow, that ending is awesome
17. did you finish your assignment
18. write your name and the date at the top
19. do you have lunch after English
20. Meet me at the table by the window

Voice

Your tone and choice of words create the **voice** of your writing. Choose a voice that is appropriate to your purpose. Use words that show your personality and your feelings on the topic.

 Write the word that best describes the voice of each writer.

1. Do you like Mr. Cole as much as I do? He is an awesome teacher to me because he makes learning fun. He can always think of a way to make me understand science, and he never makes me feel like a dork for asking questions. His way of reviewing for tests rocks! We play games using the facts and ideas we have learned.

   formal   informal

2. Members of the Awards Committee:

   I would like to nominate Ms. Mason for the Smithfield Teacher of the Year Award. She works very hard to teach us to read and write. She is always helpful and friendly. Her students respect her because she respects them.

   serious   funny

3. Wow! I just love these fast-food meals! The chicken pops taste like deep fried cotton balls. Is that pudding pop really melted chocolate rubber? My favorites are fries. Yum. They substituted sawdust for the potatoes. What creative cooking! I can't wait to go back for more.

   sarcastic respectful

 Write several sentences about a funny experience you have had. Choose words and a style that create a humorous voice.

Character Sketch

A **character sketch** makes a person or story character come alive for the reader. It includes details that describe the person's looks and personality. It points out qualities and actions that set the person apart.

First two sentences summarize important traits of the character.

Detail sentences describe the character, creating a picture.

Last sentences of paragraphs 1 and 3 show writer's feelings and establish voice.

Topic sentences of paragraphs 2 and 3 indicate the focus of these paragraphs.

A Giant of a Teacher

There is more to Mrs. Granger than meets the eye. She seems old-fashioned and strict but is really smart and funny. Everything about her is tidy and no-nonsense. She always wears a formal skirt, jacket, and blouse. She is so serious about teaching, she hasn't missed a day in years. At first I thought she was just stern and unfriendly, but I got a pleasant surprise!

Although she is tiny, Mrs. Granger seems giant to students. Her sharp gray eyes seem all-powerful. Her "X-ray vision" allows her to detect students with gum at fifty feet. Mrs. Granger makes her language arts students learn dozens of words "by the book"—the dictionary, that is!

At the same time, Mrs. Granger gives us glimpses of fun and humor. Her eyes twinkle when she tells funny jokes. What happens to the unlucky kid caught chewing gum? She sticks gum onto a card and pins it on a student's shirt. Best of all, she sees right through Nick's homework-stopping trick and turns the tables on him. I think Mrs. Granger's fifth-grade students will have a year to remember!

Subjects and Predicates

Every sentence has a subject and a predicate. The words that tell whom or what the sentence is about are the **complete subject**. The most important word in the complete subject is the **simple subject**. It is usually a noun or a pronoun. Some simple subjects have more than one word, such as *United States*.

A gentle <u>lullaby</u> relaxes everyone.
The simple subject is *lullaby*.

The words that tell what the subject is or does are the **complete predicate**. The most important word in the complete predicate is the **simple predicate**, or the verb. Some simple predicates have more than one word, such as *is walking*.

My aunt <u>plays</u> <u>lullabies on the piano</u>.
The simple predicate is *plays*.

A **fragment** is a group of words that lacks a subject or a predicate. The fragment below lacks a predicate.

The power of music.

A **run-on** is two or more complete sentences run together.

Our whole family loves music we attend many concerts.

A Write the sentence. Divide the complete subject and complete predicate with a line. Underline the simple subject once. Underline the simple predicate twice.

1. Many babies respond well to music.
2. Little babies can learn a lot.
3. I practice the piano every afternoon.
4. All people can enjoy good music.

B Identify the part of the sentence that is underlined. Write *CS* for a complete subject, *SS* for a simple subject, *CP* for a complete predicate, or *SP* for a simple predicate.

1. <u>Most parents</u> watch their babies with amazement.

2. Every new <u>accomplishment</u> by a newborn is a miracle.

3. The first smile from the baby <u>is thrilling for a parent</u>.

4. Soon a baby <u>can make</u> many sounds.

5. The new <u>parents</u> treasure every "first."

6. They <u>may write each one in a book</u>.

7. <u>Many babies</u> can say words between ages one and two.

8. By then, most babies <u>are walking</u> too.

9. <u>They</u> are racing off to school soon.

10. <u>That five years of growth</u> is astonishing.

C Write *F* for a fragment. Write *RO* for a run-on sentence. Then rewrite each item. Correct the run-ons by writing them as two separate sentences. Add words to the fragments to make sentences.

11. Children are part of the family they should help their parents.

12. Can clean their rooms.

13. Also will pick up their toys.

14. Kitchen duty can be fun many children are good cooks.

15. Eat and play together too.

Test Preparation

✔ Write the letter of the choice that shows the simple subject and simple predicate of each sentence.

1. Our whole class loves tall tales.

   A Our whole
   B class loves
   C whole class
   D loves tall tales

2. My personal favorite is *John Henry*.

   A personal favorite
   B My is
   C favorite is
   D is *John Henry*

3. John Henry worked on the railroad.

   A worked railroad
   B on the railroad
   C worked on
   D John Henry worked

4. This big man had great strength and determination.

   A man had
   B had great
   C great strength
   D big man had great

5. The railroad worker drove steel spikes with a hammer.

   A railroad worker
   B steel spikes
   C drove spikes
   D worker drove

6. A new machine could drive steel spikes.

   A machine
   B steel spikes
   C machine could drive
   D could drive steel

✔ Write the letter of the complete sentence.

7. A John Henry competed against the machine.

   B Replaced by a machine.
   C Wanted to show his worth to the railroad.
   D The powerful steel driver.

8. A Worked side by side for a long time.

   B Poured from John Henry.
   C The machine finally broke down.
   D Proved his point but died.

Review

 Write each sentence. Underline the simple subject once. Underline the simple predicate twice.

1. My brother builds things with wood.
2. Last weekend, he made a cool bird feeder.
3. It looks something like a tray.
4. Birds of all kinds are visiting it now.
5. My projects often fail miserably.
6. The hammer is not my friend.
7. Once I hit my thumb with the hammer.
8. That birdhouse on the shelf is mine.
9. No self-respecting bird would build a nest in it.
10. My mechanical creations, on the other hand, are spectacular.
11. The clock is hanging on the wall in my bedroom.
12. The proud creator admires it every day.

 Write *S* if a group of words is a sentence. Write *F* if it is a sentence fragment. Write *RO* if it is a run-on sentence.

13. Talked endlessly about the weather.
14. People can do little about it, though.
15. Meteorology is the science of weather we depend on meteorologists.
16. We cannot change the weather they can predict it.
17. Advance warning of storms.
18. People can protect themselves from the worst weather.
19. Tornadoes and hurricanes.
20. Fewer deaths from these storms today.

Creating Mood

The **mood** of a piece of writing is the feeling it creates in the reader. The writer's tone (for example, serious or playful, humorous or sad) helps establish the mood. Details that describe the setting, events, and characters also establish mood. For example, in a tall tale, exaggerations add to the humorous mood.

 Read each set of details for a story. Write the letter of the word that best describes the mood.

> **A** dignified　　**B** suspenseful　　**C** playful

1. • big, deserted mansion on a hill
   • pitch-black night with thunder
   • two kids lost inside
   • serious tone
2. • mountains that reach the sun
   • rain that makes a lake of Texas
   • cowboy who slurps it up and spits it in the ocean
   • colorful, humorous tone
3. • Native American tribal council
   • people in traditional dress
   • holding a naming ceremony for a child
   • thoughtful tone

 Write the kind of mood that you think fits these story details. Then write several sentences that establish this mood.

> tall tale about PC, a computer whiz

Tall Tale

A **tall tale** tells about the accomplishments of a larger-than-life character. It uses exaggeration to show the character's amazing abilities and to create humor. Colorful details and comparisons create vivid pictures of the fantastic events.

Mortimer Becomes a Star

The day we got Mortimer, we knew he was a special dog. Though he was just a pup, he was six feet tall and weighed 300 pounds. When he wagged his adorable tail, he cleared the furniture out of the living room. With one swipe of his tongue, he gave you a bath from head to toe.

When Mortimer outgrew the garage, we made him a bed in the barn, using 100 bales of soft, fluffy straw. Feeding him was a problem, since he ate a 50-pound bag of chow for breakfast. When he got thirsty, he lapped up the whole fish pond.

What could we do? Everyone in the family loved Mortimer. He was sweet and gentle as a baby bunny. But he was eating us out of house and home. Then a van drove up the drive. It said *Wonderful Wilbur's Pet Food* on the side.

Now that Mortimer is spokes-dog for Wonderful Wilbur's, he gets all the food he could ever want— free. He loves having a fan club!

Exaggeration sets a humorous tone.

Details create a vivid picture.

Comparison helps create mood.

Independent and Dependent Clauses

A related group of words with a subject and a predicate is called a **clause**. A clause that makes sense by itself is an **independent clause**. A clause that does not make sense by itself is a **dependent clause**. A **complex sentence** contains an independent and a dependent clause.

Independent Clause   **Dependent Clause**
↓   ↓

They lived on the island *until they were attacked*.

In the example sentence, *They lived on the island* could stand alone as a sentence, so it is an independent clause. The second clause (*until they were attacked*) cannot stand alone. It must be combined with an independent clause to make sense, so it is a dependent clause. Dependent clauses begin with words such as *if, so, when, after, because,* and *before*.

If the dependent clause comes first, set it off with a comma: *Until they were attacked, they lived on the island.* If the independent clause is first, no comma is needed: *They lived on the island until they were attacked.*

A Write *I* if the group of words is an independent clause. Write *D* if it is a dependent clause.

1. Native Americans were self sufficient
2. before white settlers came
3. because it supplied all their needs
4. they left the land in its original condition
5. when they hunted an animal
6. they used every part of it

B Write *I* if the underlined group of words is an independent clause. Write *D* if it is a dependent clause.

1. <u>When I read a book</u>, I may daydream about the story.
2. I read many survival stories <u>because they are my favorite</u>.
3. <u>I could probably survive</u> if I lived alone on an island.
4. When my scout troop took a wilderness trip last year, <u>I learned fire building and other outdoor skills</u>.
5. <u>Before I could catch fish on my island</u>, I would need a line and a hook.
6. <u>I might sleep in a cave</u> until I could build a shelter.
7. <u>Since I am good at climbing trees</u>, I could reach coconuts.
8. After a passing ship saw my fire, <u>I would be rescued from the island</u>.

C Add an independent clause to each dependent clause to make a complex sentence. Add capital letters and commas as needed. Write the sentences.

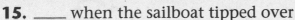

9. when my family visited a tropical island ___
10. since Mom loves the water and underwater exploring ___
11. because he is interested in surfing ___
12. ___ after I had lunch
13. ___ until the sun set
14. before we left the island ___
15. ___ when the sailboat tipped over

Test Preparation

Write the letter of the sentence that contains both an independent and a dependent clause.

1.
  A Some islands are built by volcanoes.
  B These islands grow as lava cools and hardens.
  C Such islands can be dangerous homes.
  D Volcanic eruptions cause chaos.

2.
  A A volcano may be dormant, or still, for years.
  B Many people are attracted by its beauty.
  C If the volcano erupts, they are trapped.
  D Deadly ash and gases may fill the air.

3.
  A Lava is the molten rock from a volcano.
  B It glows bright orange and flows downslope.
  C Streets, buildings, and vehicles may be destroyed.
  D After it cools, lava becomes a porous kind of rock.

4.
  A In a few years, plants sprout in rock crevices.
  B Animals come along and live off the plants.
  C When people see the island, it looks inviting.
  D It has green forests, swift streams, and colorful animals.

5.
  A However, the volcano may "blow its stack" again.
  B Geologists monitor the volcano carefully.
  C Their equipment senses when eruptions are coming.
  D Island residents can be warned ahead of time.

Review

 Write *I* for each independent clause. Write *D* for each dependent clause.

1. a shipwrecked person must be independent
2. if he or she wants to survive
3. this person cannot depend on stores for supplies
4. because there are no buildings
5. we are spoiled by the conveniences all around us
6. until we must meet a challenge like this
7. we have no idea
8. whether we could survive
9. it is rough for a softie like me
10. when the movie rental store is closed

 Write each sentence. Underline the dependent clause in each sentence.

11. Pioneers met many challenges as they moved west.
12. After they crossed the Mississippi, they were in wilderness.
13. Because there would be no towns, they brought supplies of all kinds.
14. When they saw game, they hunted for food.
15. This meat supplemented their supplies until they could buy more.
16. Since they were on their own, pioneers had to be resourceful.
17. After they settled on their land, they quickly planted crops for food.
18. Pioneers were self-sufficient because they had no other choice.

Transitions

Transitions are words or phrases that connect sentences or paragraphs. They show how one thought leads to the next.

- Some transitions help show the order, or sequence, of events: *first, next, then.*
- Some transitions describe where one place is in relationship to another: *above, below, nearby.*
- Some transitions compare and contrast *(similarly, on the other hand)* or point out a cause and effect *(because, as a result).*

Write the letter of the phrase that tells the purpose of the underlined transitions.

1. The road sliced through the desert in a straight line. <u>On the horizon</u>, long ridges of sand lay like an ocean. <u>Far in the distance</u>, hazy blue mountains pointed skyward. <u>High above their peaks</u>, the sun shone down.

    A time order   **C** compare/contrast

    B place order   **D** cause and effect

2. <u>At first</u>, the snake appeared lifeless. It lay still and coiled on a large, flat rock. <u>Then</u>, as the sun rose, the air grew warmer. <u>A little later</u>, the snake uncoiled itself and tested the air with its forked tongue.

    A time order   **C** compare/contrast

    B place order   **D** cause and effect

Write several sentences comparing and contrasting two kinds of exercise, for example, swimming and hiking. Use transition words such as *like, unlike, although, but*, and *similarly*.

Friendly or Thank-you Letter

A **friendly** or **thank-you letter** can tell about a place or events that the writer has experienced. Vivid descriptions can bring the place or events to life. Sentences and paragraphs are sometimes organized in time or place order.

Descriptive details create a picture of the scene.

Transition makes clear when the event took place. Sentence sets the scene.

Writer's excitement comes through. He describes the activity clearly.

Letter to Grandpa

Dear Grandpa,

We arrived on the island of Tortolla yesterday. It is beautiful, and I wish you could be here to see it with us. Our hotel is right on the beach, which has the whitest sand I have ever seen. The ocean has many shades of blue, and all of them are bright.

As soon as we arrived, we took a stroll along the beach. The sun was beating down so that the sand was fiery hot. I learned to walk where the waves have cooled the sand. You would love to take your daily walk here because there are so many sea birds and other animals to see.

I can't wait for tomorrow morning. I'm going to go snorkeling! I'll wear goggles and a breathing tube so I can keep my face under water. Then I will get a good look at the bright blue and yellow fish that dart in and out of the rocks on the reef.

Love,

Henry

Compound and Complex Sentences

A **simple sentence** expresses a complete thought. It has a subject and a predicate.

Satchel Paige was a great athlete.

A **compound sentence** contains two simple sentences joined by a comma and a conjunction such as *and, but,* or *or.*

Fans waited many hours to see him, but Satch never let them down.

A **complex sentence** contains an independent clause, which can stand alone, and a dependent clause, which cannot stand alone. The clauses are joined with a word such as *if, when, because, until, before, after,* or *since.* In the following sentence, the independent clause is underlined once; the dependent clause is underlined twice.

<u>When the second baseman caught the ball</u>, <u>the Tigers made a double play</u>.

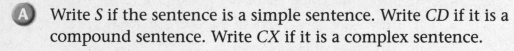 Write *S* if the sentence is a simple sentence. Write *CD* if it is a compound sentence. Write *CX* if it is a complex sentence.

1. Chele is the pitcher for the Leland Lions.
2. When she pitches, they usually win.
3. This outstanding young player has a most unusual style.
4. She winds up ten times, and then she lets it fly.
5. Her pitches look odd, but fans aren't laughing.
6. Since she gets results, they cheer her on.
7. If you go to a game, you will agree.
8. Chele's talent may earn her a scholarship.

B Write each sentence. Underline the word that joins the two clauses in each sentence. Write *CD* if the sentence is a compound sentence. Write *CX* if it is a complex sentence.

1. Many sports heroes have unusual nicknames, but these nicknames are used with affection.

2. Leroy Paige was called Satchel because he carried baggage as a boy.

3. "Babe" is a famous sports nickname, and many players have had it.

4. Do you think first of Babe Ruth, or does the name Babe Didrikson Zaharias come to mind?

5. If I were a star, I would choose the nickname "Magic."

C Join each pair of simple sentences with the conjunction in ( ). Write the compound or complex sentence. Change punctuation and capital letters as necessary.

6. Sports heroes are larger than life. Fans feel close to them. (but)

7. Fans read stories and articles about their favorite. They wear clothing with that star's name and number. (and)

8. A sports hero is playing. Fans always watch the game. (when)

9. Satchel Paige was a player in the major leagues. He was a star in the Negro Leagues. (before)

10. Paige pitched superbly. He also brought out huge crowds. (and)

11. Paige turned 59 in 1965. He became the oldest pitcher in the major leagues. (when)

12. Satchel Paige died in 1982. His legend will live forever. (but)

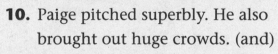

Test Preparation

Write the letter of the phrase that correctly identifies each underlined word, group of words, or sentence.

1. <u>If you join our baseball team</u>, you will have a good time.

   A dependent clause
   B simple sentence
   C compound sentence
   D complex sentence

2. James is usually the catcher, <u>but</u> he may play first base.

   A conjunction
   B simple sentence
   C compound sentence
   D complex sentence

3. <u>We don't always win, but we do enjoy the game</u>.

   A dependent clause
   B simple sentence
   C compound sentence
   D complex sentence

4. <u>If we have had a good time, we are happy</u>.

   A dependent clause
   B simple sentence
   C compound sentence
   D complex sentence

5. Mr. Jennings is a good coach <u>because he doesn't yell</u>.

   A dependent clause
   B simple sentence
   C compound sentence
   D complex sentence

6. <u>He always encourages us and explains our mistakes</u>.

   A dependent clause
   B simple sentence
   C compound sentence
   D complex sentence

Review

Join each pair of simple sentences using the conjunction in ( ). Write the compound sentence with correct capitalization and punctuation.

1. My family enjoys all kinds of sports.
We play together every weekend. (and)

2. In summer, we play baseball in the park.
We set up the volleyball net in the yard. (or)

3. My favorite sport is basketball.
Ice hockey is a close second. (but)

4. My older brother runs on a track team.
He has become much faster this year. (and)

5. I will join the team.
I will have to wait a few years. (but)

Write each sentence. Underline the word that joins the two clauses in each sentence. Write *CD* if the sentence is a compound sentence. Write *CX* if it is a complex sentence.

6. African Americans formed the Negro Leagues because they were barred from the major leagues.

7. The Negro League players were just as talented, and they thrilled their fans just as much as the major league players.

8. When the Negro Leagues were in full swing, Satchel Paige was its most famous player.

9. Paige drew huge crowds before he became a major league player.

10. He made more money than any other African American player of the time, and he traveled around the world.

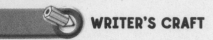

Tone

A writer's **tone** expresses an attitude toward the subject. Word choice, sentence structure, and word pictures made by details and comparisons create the tone in a piece of writing.

 Write a word from the box to describe the tone of each passage.

humorous	admiring	disapproving

1. Babe Didrikson Zaharias excelled at every sport—and she tried them all! Her greatest claims to fame were as a track star and a superb golfer. Babe qualified in five events for the 1932 Olympics and won 55 golf tournaments. Her humor and self-confidence brought her a special place in sports history.

2. The argument on the field at Hall Park last night is a model of bad sportsmanship. Several students booed the umpire's call of strike three. One even ran onto the diamond and argued with the umpire. This behavior is childish and silly.

3. My cat Pickles is a pain! I can call and call her. Just when I think she's lost, injured, or kidnapped, she ambles in, yawning and blinking innocently as if to say, "Were you calling me?" On the other hand, who else makes me laugh until I cry with her antics over a catnip mouse?

 Write a paragraph about an interesting or unusual person. Use words, sentence structures, and descriptive details that create a suitable tone.

Feature Article

A **feature article** tells about an interesting person or experience. It answers the questions *Who? What? When? Where? Why?* It grabs your attention at the beginning. Descriptive details and facts provide information about the person or experience.

Details paint a vivid picture and make an attention-grabbing opener.

Facts answer who, what, when, where, and why.

Word choices add to picture of Goodall's personality.

Jane Goodall

Jane Goodall's favorite kind of day begins very early in the African forest. She follows a chimpanzee mother and her family. This means climbing high, far, and fast. It also means hours of crawling on her belly with vines catching her hair. At dusk, she will be exhausted, bruised, and very happy.

Jane Goodall began her amazing study of African chimpanzees in 1960 when she was 26. Even as a little girl, Jane knew she must somehow "find a way to watch free, wild animals living their own undisturbed lives."

At first, the chimps ran whenever they saw Jane. Patient and determined, Jane did not give up. As time passed, the chimps let her get closer. She learned amazing new things about them. For example, she was the first to see that they used tools. She was the first to understand that they have lasting family relationships.

Today, Jane's heroic work is recognized around the world. She has labored tirelessly to save chimpanzees, which have become endangered. Her efforts have improved the environment for all living things.

Common and Proper Nouns

The names of particular persons, places, and things are **proper nouns**. Capitalize the first word and each important word of a proper noun.

Alexi Bishop lives in Seattle, Washington.

All other nouns are **common nouns**. They are not capitalized.

Our family has lived in the city and on the coast.

Capitalize the first word and all important words in a title.

Have you read *The Wind in the Willows*?

Capitalize days of the week and months of the year.

Class meets on Mondays in May.

Capitalize the first letter of an abbreviated proper noun. Abbreviations often occur in addresses, titles in names, and names of days and months. An initial is a type of abbreviation. Most abbreviations end with a period.

The envelope went to Ms. M. R. Ryan, 1410 Montgomery St., Raleigh, NC 27607. It was postmarked Wed., Sept. 27.

A If the group of words is capitalized correctly, write *correct*. If the group of words is not capitalized correctly, rewrite it using correct capitalization.

1. 1234 north First ave., oshkosh, WI
2. my aunt col. t. zena Smith
3. a meeting on tues., Jan. 18
4. his new book *my Journey To Africa*
5. our neighbor Ms. Carmen w. ruiz

B Write *P* if the list shows proper nouns. Write *C* if the list shows common nouns. Then add another example to each list.

1. baseball, basketball, football
2. New York, Miami, Phoenix
3. April, July, September
4. infants, toddlers, teenagers
5. Fifth Ave., Main St., Monroe Blvd.
6. aunts, cousins, grandparents
7. Friday, Monday, Wednesday
8. Mr., Dr., Sen.

C Write each sentence, capitalizing all proper nouns.

9. Living in a big city such as los angeles or detroit can be exciting.
10. It is also more stressful than living in a small town in the south.
11. Tourists visit sites such as chicago's art institute or new york's museum of modern art.
12. They also love remote attractions such as mount rushmore and yellowstone national park.
13. You have an appointment on monday, october 17, with dr. umesh r. goswami.
14. His office is at 1142 north jefferson ave., suite 101.
15. He has hung pictures of president abraham lincoln in the waiting room, and the song "america the beautiful" is playing.

Test Preparation

 Write the letter of the answer that is correctly capitalized.

1. A senator julia weisman
   B senator Julia Weisman
   C Senator Julia Weisman
   D Senator julia Weisman

2. A 907 south Third st.
   B 907 South Third St.
   C 907 South Third st.
   D 907 south third st.

3. A *My Side of the Mountain*
   B *My Side Of The Mountain*
   C *My side of the Mountain*
   D *My side of the mountain*

4. A Field Museum of natural History
   B field Museum of Natural History
   C Field Museum Of Natural History
   D Field Museum of Natural History

5. A james d. ellis, sr.
   B James D. Ellis, Sr.
   C James D. Ellis, sr.
   D James d. Ellis, Sr.

6. A Monday, November 22
   B monday, November 22
   C Monday, november 22
   D monday, november 22

7. A lynchburg, VA 24502
   B Lynchburg, Va 24502
   C Lynchburg, va 24502
   D Lynchburg, VA 24502

8. A the movie *Snow white and the seven Dwarfs*
   B the Movie *Snow White and the Seven Dwarfs*
   C the movie *Snow White and the Seven Dwarfs*
   D the movie *Snow White And The Seven Dwarfs*

Review

✓ Write *C* if the group of words is capitalized correctly. If the group of words is not capitalized correctly, rewrite it using correct capitalization.

1. tokyo, Japan
2. Mr. Jack Goodrich
3. Mario and his Friends
4. on thursday, january 20
5. skyscrapers in Dallas, texas
6. Gold beach, or 97444
7. a Street near our Street
8. Pacific Ocean
9. independence Day
10. *Oliver Twist* by Charles Dickens

✓ Rewrite each sentence. Use capital letters where they are needed.

11. On vacation we drove across iowa, nebraska, colorado, and wyoming.
12. I especially liked rocky mountain national park.
13. We live in the midwest, but we often visit new england.
14. Much of our country's history is centered in boston and philadelphia.
15. Have you seen faneuil hall or the liberty bell?
16. *Johnny tremain* is a novel about the revolutionary war in america.
17. The united states army was led by commander-in-chief George washington.
18. Please send the book to wayne j. yates, jr., 5039 west donnybrook lane, enid, ok 73703.

Show, Don't Tell

> When you write about yourself, **show—don't tell—** how you feel.
>
> **No**   I felt relieved.
>
> **Yes**   I let out a huge breath and leaned back. I felt the knots in my stomach relax.

 Circle the letter of the sentence ending that shows rather than tells.

1. The city skyline

  A rose into the clouds, glittering like jewels.

  B was inspiring.

2. Overhead, the sun

  A was shining brightly.

  B dazzled and warmed me with its brilliance.

3. Rush hour traffic

  A had slowed down quite a bit.

  B inched along at an agonizing pace.

4. Exhaust fumes

  A fouled the air with the raw smell of gasoline.

  B smelled strong and unpleasant.

 Imagine that you have just walked into a new classroom. You don't know anyone. Write about this experience. Show, don't tell, what the room is like and how you feel.

Writing for Tests

Prompt Tell about a time when you got <u>something you treasured</u>. What effect did it have on you? Write a <u>narrative</u> to a <u>friend</u> telling how you made this treasure your own and how you felt. Remember to indent each new paragraph.

Specific details, comparisons, and strong verbs create vivid images.

Writer shows how she feels.

Writer uses a figure of speech to show feelings.

The Snuggles Sale

I knew when I saw him, he had to be mine. The little gerbil had soft gray fur. A white stripe on his nose looked like an exclamation mark. He gave me a careful sniff—his whiskers tickled my fingers! I cuddled him in my hands and immediately felt that warm puppy feeling. But could Mom be convinced? My heart went from warm to chill.

"Look, Mom," I said, lifting my hands. "This is Snuggles. He's a gerbil. Feel how soft!" I moved a finger just enough, and the tiny face with bright eyes popped into view. "Isn't he the cutest thing you've ever seen?" I said. Mom smiled uncertainly.

"Please, Mom," I talked fast. "I'll take care of Snuggles. He can live in my room. I can use the old aquarium for his home. Gerbils are very clean. He won't be underfoot, and he won't bark and he doesn't need to be walked or— "

Soon we were on the way home, with Snuggles exploring happily in my jacket. My heart bubbled like a glass of soda.

Regular and Irregular Plural Nouns

Plural nouns name more than one person, place, or thing.

- Add *-s* to form the plural of most nouns.
  picture/pictures   wing/wings   pattern/patterns

- Add *-es* to nouns ending in *ch, sh, x, z, s,* and *ss.*
  bunch/bunches   wish/wishes
  box/boxes   class/classes

- If a noun ends in a vowel and *y,* add *-s.*
  day/days   boy/boys

- If a noun ends in a consonant and *y,*
  change *y* to *i* and add *-es.*
  city/cities   lady/ladies

- Some nouns have **irregular plural** forms. They change
  spelling.
  man/men   mouse/mice   goose/geese
  foot/feet   child/children

- For most nouns that end in *f* or *fe,* change *f* to *v* and add *-es.*
  leaf/leaves   knife/knives   calf/calves

- Some nouns have the same singular and plural forms.
  sheep   deer   moose   headquarters   series

A Write the plural form of each noun. Use a dictionary if you
need help.

1. wish
2. grasshopper
3. shelf
4. Saturday
5. hunch

6. hoax
7. deer
8. dime
9. paper
10. gallery

B Write the plural forms of the underlined singular nouns.

1. Child who can speak two language are bilingual.

2. Sara can name several fruit, vegetable, and animal in Spanish.

3. What do you call butterfly, leaf, and branch in Spanish?

4. Several woman brought English-Spanish dictionary.

5. We learned the difference between horse, pony, and donkey.

6. Buy two bunch of banana, some strawberry, and peach for the salad.

7. Cut the melon in two half, and then remove the seed.

8. Serve the salad in unusual dish or glass with sprig of mint.

9. Shall we use the bowl with goose on it or the one with sheep on it?

10. Spanish-speaking family enjoy the community dinner on Friday.

C Write each sentence. Correct any errors in plural forms of nouns.

11. Fifth-grade classs bought lunchs for childs who were hungry.

12. Studentes had asked about wayes they could make a difference in their communitys.

13. They also collected cannes of food and made up boxies for food pantrys.

14. Our class had bake sals to raise money for flood victimz.

15. Look around. You will find many adults, boyes, and girls whose lifes could be improved.

Test Preparation

✓ Write the letter of the plural word that correctly completes each sentence.

1. Do you know how to care for your ____ properly?

    A tooths   **C** teeth
    B tooth   **D** teeths

2. Some ____ are too hard or too soft.

    A toothbrushes
    B teethbrush
    C toothbrushs
    D teethbrushes

3. Brush three ____ a day.

    A timez   **C** tims
    B times   **D** timeys

4. Avoid eating between ____.

    A meales   **C** meal
    B mealles   **D** meals

5. Wild ____ do not follow these tips.

    A animals   **C** animales
    B animalles   **D** animalz

6. Try to imagine ____ brushing their fangs.

    A wolvies   **C** wolfs
    B wolves   **D** wolfes

7. Can you picture ____ getting a filling?

    A oxes   **C** ox
    B oxs   **D** oxen

8. ____ and zoo animals get oral care.

    A Pets   **C** Petes
    B Petts   **D** Petz

9. Wild cats and ____ live longer with healthy mouths.

    A sheepz   **C** sheep
    B sheepes   **D** sheeps

10. Don't eat ____; they will stain.

    A cherris   **C** cherrys
    B cherryes   **D** cherries

Review

 Write the plural form of each singular noun listed.

1. crutch	**11.** box
2. bridge	**12.** headquarters
3. fly	**13.** peach
4. kiss	**14.** desk
5. question	**15.** wife
6. leaf	**16.** lady
7. blackberry	**17.** goose
8. deer	**18.** dish
9. turkey	**19.** series
10. man	**20.** key

 Write each sentence. Correct any errors in plural forms of nouns.

21. It's better to have friendz than enemys.

22. I sometimes have argumenties with my pales.

23. Javier wants to change the rulz to gams we play.

24. Try to resolve your differenceses without conflictes.

25. We should try to avoid stresss in our lifes.

26. This goes for childrens as well as mans and womans.

27. Anger and worryes are thiefs that rob us of the simple joyz in life.

28. Do you see any foxs, mooses, monkies, or mouses wasting time on worry?

29. Staying mad at otherz is less fun than pulling tooths.

30. Admit your part in causing problemes, and then let go of bad feelinges.

Eliminate Wordiness

Express your ideas clearly and directly. To **eliminate wordiness,** delete words that repeat or are unnecessary. Replace wordy phrases with specific words.

Wordy	He was often late and not on time.
Improved	He was often late.
Wordy	He wore a coat that had many colors.
Improved	He wore a colorful coat.

 Write each sentence. Leave out words that repeat or are unnecessary.

1. Patti had temper tantrums and she often cried and had a fit to get her way.

2. Her parents were upset by these tantrums and felt awful about them.

3. However, they did not reward or otherwise give in to Patti for her misbehavior.

4. They encouraged good behavior and ignored or did not pay attention to bad behavior.

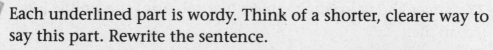 Each underlined part is wordy. Think of a shorter, clearer way to say this part. Rewrite the sentence.

5. When I see someone in trouble, I always <u>endeavor to try to stop and give them the benefit of my assistance.</u>

6. Last week, I saw a new kid in school <u>having a great deal of trouble in opening her school storage unit.</u>

7. I helped her open the locker, and then I <u>provided her with guidelines for opening it in the future.</u>

8. Helping other people makes me feel <u>a positive upswing,</u> and <u>on some occasions</u> it leads to new friendships.

Summary

> A **summary** highlights the main ideas from an article or a story. Because a summary is brief, it does not include minor details, repeated words or thoughts, or unimportant ideas. Write a summary in your own words, but do not include your opinions.

First paragraph summarizes basic information of the story.

Detail sentences reveal cleverness of main character.

Final sentence shows the outcome of the plot.

Story Summary: The Three Little Pigs

A mother pig sends her three young pigs out into the world, telling them to build a safe house to keep out the wolf. The first little pig builds a house of straw, the second builds a house of sticks, and the third builds a house of bricks.

The wolf easily blows down the straw house and eats the first little pig. The second pig and his stick house suffer the same fate. When he cannot blow down the brick house, the wolf tries to trick the third little pig. The wolf invites the pig to go with him to several different events. Each time, however, the clever little pig goes earlier than the appointed time and returns home safely.

The enraged wolf tries to enter the brick house through the chimney. However, the pig outwits him again by capturing the wolf in a pot of boiling water and scalding him to death.

Possessive Nouns

A **possessive noun** shows ownership. A **singular possessive** noun shows that one person, place, or thing has or owns something. A **plural possessive noun** shows that more than one person, place, or thing has or owns something.

- To make a singular noun show possession, add an apostrophe (') and -s.
  the baby's crib
- To make a plural noun that ends in -s show possession, add an apostrophe (').
  the soldiers' uniforms
- To make a plural noun that does not end in -s show possession, add an apostrophe (') and -s.
  the men's shoes

A Write the possessive form of each singular and plural noun.

1. family
2. brother
3. suitcase
4. child
5. government
6. pen
7. train
8. tree
9. woman
10. refugee

11. families
12. brothers
13. suitcases
14. children
15. governments
16. pens
17. trains
18. trees
19. women
20. refugees

B Write each noun as a possessive noun. Write *S* if the possessive noun is singular. Write *P* if the possessive noun is plural.

1. ponies
2. army
3. windows
4. basket
5. grandfather
6. birds
7. glass
8. schools
9. teeth
10. pennies
11. nurse
12. wings
13. man
14. general
15. colonies

C Add an apostrophe (') or an apostrophe (') and -*s* to make each underlined word possessive. Then write a sentence using the phrase.

16. every <u>person</u> right
17. <u>America</u> Declaration of Independence
18. <u>Thomas Jefferson</u> work
19. <u>men</u> signatures
20. our <u>nation</u> ideas
21. <u>children</u> freedom
22. most <u>nations</u> goals
23. some <u>leaders</u> motives
24. a <u>dictator</u> greed
25. the <u>United Nations</u> role

Test Preparation

✔ Write the letter of the word that correctly completes each sentence.

1. During war, all _____ lives are disrupted.

   A peoples   C citizen's
   B citizen   D citizens'

2. A _____ violence leaves death and destruction behind.

   A war's   C wars'
   B war   D wars

3. A _____ duty is to protect his or her country.

   A soldiers   C soldiers'
   B soldier's   D soldier

4. Soldiers must follow _____ orders.

   A officers   C officer
   B officer's   D officers'

5. One _____ farm was totally destroyed in battle.

   A man's   C mens'
   B mans   D mans'

6. All the _____ lives must be spared.

   A prisoners   C prisoner
   B prisoners'   D prisoner's

7. A _____ idea is to avoid war.

   A pacifists'   C pacifist
   B pacifists   D pacifist's

8. Any war puts people in _____ way.

   A harms   C harm's
   B harms'   D harm

9. Peace is in the whole _____ best interests.

   A world's   C world
   B worlds'   D worlds

10. Some _____ leaders don't understand this, however.

   A countries   C countrie's
   B countries'   D country

Review

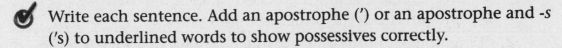 Write the possessive form of each noun. Write *S* if it is a singular possessive. Write *P* if it is a plural possessive.

1. backpack	**11.** gentlemen
2. sleds	**12.** sheep
3. mice	**13.** books
4. cows	**14.** dress
5. buses	**15.** teeth
6. vest	**16.** turkey
7. letters	**17.** box
8. story	**18.** women
9. lesson	**19.** children
10. child	**20.** deer

Write each sentence. Add an apostrophe (') or an apostrophe and -*s* ('s) to underlined words to show possessives correctly.

21. <u>Slaves</u> lives were terribly hard.

22. They were at the mercy of <u>owners</u> whims.

23. A <u>runaway</u> life was in danger.

24. Often runaways traveled by the <u>moon</u> light.

25. It could take several <u>weeks</u> travel to reach the North.

26. Slaves hid directions in a <u>song</u> words.

27. <u>Abolitionists</u> role was to hide and help runaways.

28. A safe house meant a <u>night</u> rest in a bed and a hot meal.

29. A <u>stranger</u> kindness lifted the <u>runaways</u> spirits.

30. Many runaways stopped only when they reached <u>Canada</u> free soil.

Support Your Ideas

> When you give an opinion about a story, you should **support your ideas** with facts and details. These details can include examples and quotes from the story or descriptions of characters or actions.

 Read each opinion. Write the letters of the sentences that help support this opinion.

1. Cinderella is mistreated by her stepfamily.

   A She does all the hard, unpleasant work.

   B She gets poor food and clothing.

   C Her stepmother and stepsisters make fun of her.

   D She runs from the prince at midnight.

2. "King Midas and the Golden Touch" shows that love is more valuable than gold.

   A King Midas changes everything he touches to gold.

   B King Midas hates his power when it costs him his beloved daughter.

   C King Midas loves gold more than anything.

   D King Midas offers to give up everything to get his daughter back.

3. King Midas loves his daughter very much.

   A He always wants to make her happy.

   B King Midas changes his daughter to a gold statue.

   C He is sorrowful when she is a statue.

   D He takes steps to remove his "golden curse" and cure his daughter.

 Write your opinion about an important idea in a story you have read. List at least three pieces of evidence from the story that support your opinion.

Story Review

A **story review** tells readers about a story's theme, setting, and characters and gives a brief summary of its plot. A review is also a critique because it tells the writer's thoughts and opinions about the story. These ideas should be supported by details from the story.

Story Review: Goldilocks and the Three Bears

First paragraph describes Goldilocks's character and the setting.

Goldilocks is a mischievous girl who discovers a house in the woods and cannot resist going in. The owners are out for a walk, but Goldilocks doesn't let that stop her.

Details tell about the plot.

Everything is laid out in threes. Goldilocks tries the three bowls of porridge; then she eats the porridge in the teeny tiny bowl. Next, she tries the three chairs. She likes the teeny tiny one best, but she breaks it. Then she tries out the three beds and falls asleep in the teeny tiny one.

The owners—a family of bears—return home and are alarmed about the break-in. Poor baby bear's breakfast is eaten, his chair is broken, and his bed is still occupied by Goldilocks! She wakes, sees the bears, and runs for all she is worth. It serves her right to be frightened, I say, because she was thoughtless to meddle in a stranger's house.

Writer provides an opinion and the reason for it.

Action and Linking Verbs

A complete sentence has a subject and a predicate. The main word in the predicate is a verb. An **action verb** tells what the subject does.

The river *floods* the town.

Action verbs can tell about actions that are physical *(walk, carry)* or mental *(forget, understand)*.

A **linking verb** links, or joins, the subject to a word or words in the predicate. It tells what the subject is or is like.

The townspeople *are* afraid.

Forms of the verb *be (am, is, are, was, were)* are often used as linking verbs.

These verbs also can be linking verbs: *become, seem, appear, feel, taste, smell,* and *look. (I feel hungry. The pie smells delicious.)* However, some of them can also be used as action verbs. *(Feel this fabric. The dog smells many scents.)*

A Write the verb in each sentence. Write *A* if it is an action verb. Write *L* if it is a linking verb.

1. The girl feels nervous.
2. Today is her wedding day.
3. She sits in a fancy chair.
4. Footmen carry the chair on their shoulders.
5. Her parents arranged the marriage.
6. She is only sixteen years old.
7. She sees her husband for the first time.
8. He looks handsome and kind.
9. She appears happy and content.
10. The families hope for a happy marriage.

B Write the verb from each sentence. Write *MA* if it shows mental action. Write *PA* if it shows physical action. Write *L* if it is a linking verb.

1. A wedding day is special everywhere in the world.
2. Different cultures believe different things about marriage.
3. In some countries, a bride gives a dowry.
4. The dowry is money and goods for the husband or his family.
5. In other countries, the husband and wife live with his family.
6. Almost always, wedding guests feast.
7. The bride and groom dress in splendid clothes.
8. All the guests look joyful.
9. The husband and wife open many gifts.
10. Their friends and relatives are generous.
11. They want a happy, properous life for the newlyweds.
12. Everywhere, a marriage is a festive occasion.

C Add a verb of your own to complete each sentence. Write the sentence. Then write *A* or *L* to tell what kind of verb each one is.

13. A little brown dog ____ on our doorstep.
14. Clearly, it ____ lost.
15. My brother ____ it Brewster.
16. Mom ____ a notice in the papers and stores.
17. We ____ quite fond of Brewster.
18. Then one day, Brewster's owners ____.
19. Brewster ____ overjoyed!
20. We ____ sad for ourselves but glad for Brewster.

Test Preparation

✓ Write the letter of the phrase that correctly identifies the underlined word in the sentence.

1. In China, shrines <u>honor</u> ancestors.

    A action verb (physical)
    B action verb (mental)
    C linking verb
    D not a verb

2. A shrine <u>is</u> a sacred place.

    A action verb (physical)
    B action verb (mental)
    C linking verb
    D not a verb

3. Visitors <u>meditate</u> at the shrine.

    A action verb (physical)
    B action verb (mental)
    C linking verb
    D not a verb

4. They also <u>burn</u> incense.

    A action verb (physical)
    B action verb (mental)
    C linking verb
    D not a verb

5. The incense <u>smells</u> smoky and fragrant.

    A action verb (physical)
    B action verb (mental)
    C linking verb
    D not a verb

6. Descendants <u>gaze</u> at pictures and possessions of the ancestors.

    A action verb (physical)
    B action verb (mental)
    C linking verb
    D not a verb

7. In America, we visit the <u>graves</u> of loved ones.

    A action verb (physical)
    B action verb (mental)
    C linking verb
    D not a verb

8. We <u>place</u> flowers on the grave.

    A action verb (physical)
    B action verb (mental)
    C linking verb
    D not a verb

Review

 Write the verb in each sentence. Write *A* if it is an action verb. Write *L* if it is a linking verb.

1. Rita learned a lesson about generosity.
2. Grandma sent her several birthday gifts.
3. Her favorite was a pair of skates.
4. She also loved the game and book.
5. That day she met a needy family.
6. Their daughter looked ten or eleven.
7. Unlike Rita, this girl had very few belongings.
8. Rita felt very sorry for her.
9. She gave the girl her new skates.
10. This act made Rita happy, not sad.
11. The girl's smile was a reward.
12. Grandma appeared proud of Rita for her unselfishness.

 Write each sentence. Add a verb from the box to make the action vivid.

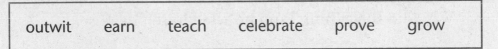

| outwit | earn | teach | celebrate | prove | grow |

13. Fairy tales _____ children about life.
14. Characters _____ wiser as a result of challenges.
15. Boys and girls _____ their intelligence and strength in the face of danger.
16. They _____ the fiercest beasts and tyrants.
17. They _____ love and wealth after great hardships.
18. Fairy tales _____ a youth's coming of age.

Answer 5 Ws and How

A news story gives key information about an event. It answers a set of questions called the **5 Ws and How:** *Who? What? Where? When? Why? How?* This essential information informs readers about the event in direct, concrete, and objective sentences.

 Read each news story lead. For each story, list the words *Who?, What?, Where?, When?, Why?,* and *How?* Then write the details that answer each question.

1. The three Porkson brothers of Curly Tale Lane narrowly avoided being eaten by a very hungry predator, B. B. Wolf, yesterday. Wolf blew down the houses of Porky and Dorky Porkson, which were made of straw and wood, respectively. The pair finally escaped to brother Gorky's brick home.

2. Notorious outlaw Gigundo Grossman was killed Friday morning when local entrepreneur Jack Climber cut down the stalk on which Grossman was climbing. Climber alleges that Grossman was "out to get him," and he acted in self-defense.

 Write a news story based on a familiar fairy tale or other story you have read. Include the basic information (5 Ws and How) from the story in your article.

News Story

> A **news story** gives the facts about an event. It focuses on answering these six questions: *Who? What? Where? When? Why?* and *How?* A good news story begins with a lead that grabs readers' attention and sets up the story. The body of the news story explains and supports the lead with specific details and examples.

Lead grabs attention and sets up the story.

Background information is provided.

Quotes engage readers and reveal motives.

Queen Saves Child, Foils Gold Scam

The Queen outwitted a man who sought to take her child as repayment for his gold-spinning services last year.

The man, who refused to give his name, tried to collect on a promise the Queen had made last year. At the time, the King had locked her in a room full of straw and demanded that she spin it into gold. Because her father had sworn she could do this, the King demanded proof.

Said the Queen, "He was a funny little man, but very talented. He demanded payment for his help, but I was quite poor. Instead, he made me promise to give him my firstborn. I never thought he'd hold me to it!"

Seeing her distress, the man offered to release the Queen from her promise if she could learn his name in three days. That name, Rumpelstiltskin, was discovered by a messenger. Upon being named, Rumpelstiltskin flew into a rage and tore himself in two.

Main and Helping Verbs

Verbs that are made up of more than one word are **verb phrases**. In a verb phrase, the **main verb** names the action. The **helping verb** helps tell the time of the action. Some common helping verbs are *has, have, had, am, is, are, was, were, be, been, do, does, did, can, could, will, would, and should.*

- The main verb is always the last word in a verb phrase. (Animals *are* <u>losing</u> habitats.)

- There may be more than one helping verb in a verb phrase. (We <u>*should have*</u> *saved* more wetland habitats.)

- Helping verbs such as *is* and *are* show that action is happening in the present. (Forests *are cut* down for wood.) *Was* and *were* show that the action happened in the past. (Once millions of acres of forest *were standing* in this area.) *Will* shows that the action is happening in the future. (Trees *will disappear* if we don't conserve them.)

A Write the verb phrase in each sentence. Underline the helping verb.

1. For years, people have given names to their pets.

2. Our dog is named Groucho.

3. Pets can perform wonderful tricks.

4. Groucho has entertained us for years.

5. He could become a standup comic.

6. Sometimes he will walk on his hind legs.

7. You should see his stubby tail.

8. No one can resist his floppy ears.

B Write the verb from each sentence. If the verb is a verb phrase, underline the helping verb twice and the main verb once.

1. The Willow Equine Rescue Barn has been helping horses in trouble.

2. Some of the horses there are suffering from injuries.

3. A few were mistreated by their owners.

4. Horses should be provided with the right food.

5. This horse will need medicine, care, and the right diet.

6. Kay and Dick have been volunteering at the Rescue Barn.

7. They can brush the horses' coats.

8. A veterinarian is examining the new arrivals.

C Notice how verbs express past, present, or future time in each underlined item. Copy the last sentence in each item. Include a verb phrase that matches the tense of the underlined verbs.

9. Five young deer are standing like statues on my lawn. They are slim and graceful. One _____ from the bird feeder.

10. In the last five years, builders put up a lot of strip malls nearby. Lots of fields and woods were covered by concrete and asphalt. Animals _____ out of their homes.

11. The loss of habitat will become a pressing issue soon. As more land is lost, wildlife will be forced to live side by side with humans. People _____ animals eating their grass and bushes.

12. I have seen many kinds of wildlife from my windows. Last week a fox trotted by. Raccoons have raided the trash cans. In the past two years, coyotes _____ many gardens.

Test Preparation

Write the letter of the words that correctly identify the underlined word or words in the sentence.

1. We <u>can help</u> wild animals in many ways.

   A helping verb
   B main verb
   C verb phrase
   D not a verb

2. We <u>should</u> recognize the importance of every animal.

   A helping verb
   B main verb
   C verb phrase
   D not a verb

3. Every animal is <u>playing</u> a role in the ecosystem.

   A helping verb
   B main verb
   C verb phrase
   D not a verb

4. Some species could be <u>eliminated</u>.

   A helping verb
   B main verb
   C verb phrase
   D not a verb

5. This will cause an <u>imbalance</u> in the ecosystem.

   A helping verb
   B main verb
   C verb phrase
   D not a verb

6. Some other animals <u>have lost</u> their food supply.

   A helping verb
   B main verb
   C verb phrase
   D not a verb

Review

 Write a helping verb from the box that can complete each sentence.

should	does	are	can	will	have been

1. _____ your community have a recycling center?
2. People in our town _____ recycle paper, glass, metal, and plastic if they want.
3. Recyclables _____ collected every Thursday by special trucks.
4. I _____ carry out the blue recycling bin after breakfast.
5. According to the guidelines, we _____ put the newspapers in paper bags.
6. The glass jars _____ washed out already.

 Write each verb phrase. Underline the helping verb or verbs twice and the main verb once.

7. I am watching a show about animals.
8. Ginny has observed them at the zoo.
9. Those monkeys are grooming one another.
10. That koala is sleeping in a tree.
11. Two colorful birds have been building a nest.
12. A giraffe has stretched its neck to the top branches.
13. Usually it would grab the highest leaves.
14. The elephants are playing in the water.
15. Their trunks can act like hoses.
16. The mother elephant has sprayed water on her baby.
17. No visitors should feed the animals at the zoo.
18. Zookeepers will give them the right food.

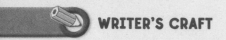

Know Your Purpose

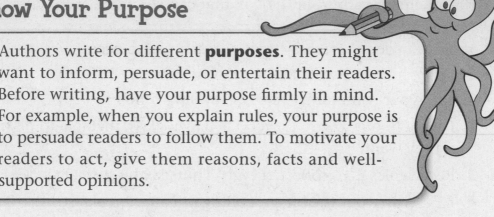

Authors write for different **purposes**. They might want to inform, persuade, or entertain their readers. Before writing, have your purpose firmly in mind. For example, when you explain rules, your purpose is to persuade readers to follow them. To motivate your readers to act, give them reasons, facts and well-supported opinions.

 Read each rule and the sentences that follow it. Write the numbers of the sentences that support the rule.

Avoid overly packaged, "disposable" products.

1. Plastic and plastic foam packaging will not break down and are not often recycled.

2. Marketers make packaging colorful and appealing.

3. "Disposable" products have to be thrown away, so they waste resources.

4. Some packaging materials, such as plastic foam, harm the environment.

Compost natural wastes.

5. Leaves and other yard waste add to the richness of the soil.

6. Putting this waste in the trash uses landfill space.

7. Burning this waste contributes to air pollution.

8. Bird feeders and birdhouses will make your yard an attractive habitat.

 Think of your own rule for saving the environment. Write your rule. Then write at least three pieces of evidence (facts, opinions, examples, or logical arguments) to show why the rule is a good one.

Rules

Some writing assignments will ask you to support your ideas with **rules**. Make sure that each rule is stated clearly and concisely and supports your main idea. Rules may consist of a simple list, or they may be developed in paragraphs with persuasive details.

Details give compelling, logical reasons to follow rules.

Rules are expressed as brief commands using specific verbs.

Exact, vivid words drive home the point and persuade readers.

Rules to Save the Environment

1. Recycle everything you can.

Think of all the paper, glass, metal, and plastic you throw out every week in the trash. These precious natural resources could be used again instead of being buried in a landfill. As garbage, they take up room and can pollute the land. If we recycle them, we will need to cut fewer trees, dig less ore, and pump less oil.

2. Conserve water every way you can.

Clean fresh water is essential to life. Earth has an enormous population of humans and a limited supply of water. When you run water needlessly, you waste our most precious resource. Take a brief shower instead of a long one. Flush the toilet less often. Fix leaky faucets. You'll be surprised how many thousands of gallons of water you save over time!

3. Use the car only when you must.

Vehicles use up Earth's oil. (Gasoline is made from oil.) Like many of Earth's resources, oil is nonrenewable. That means Earth is not making more oil—at least not fast enough for us. Also, exhaust from motors is polluting the air and contributing to global warming. Carpool, walk, bike, or use public transportation whenever possible.

Subject-Verb Agreement

The subject and verb in a sentence must **agree**, or work together. A singular subject needs a singular verb. A plural subject needs a plural verb.

Use these rules for verbs that tell about the present time.

- If the subject is a singular noun or *he, she,* or *it,* add *-s* or *-es* to most verbs.

  A horse *runs*. A dog *chases* the horse. It *barks* loudly.

- If the subject is a plural noun or *I, you, we,* or *they,* do not add *-s* or *-es* to the verb.

  Horses *run*. Dogs *chase* the horse. They *bark* loudly.

- For the verb *be,* use *am* and *is* to agree with singular subjects and *are* to agree with plural subjects.

  I *am* afraid. Paul *is* fearless. The armies *are* here. We *are* surprised.

- A collective noun names a group, such as *family, team,* and *class*. A collective noun is singular if it refers to a group acting as one: The class is *going* on a field trip. A collective noun is plural if it refers to members of the group acting individually: The class *are debating* about which place to visit.

A Write the subject of each sentence. Then write the verb in ( ) that agrees with the subject.

1. American history (is, are) an interesting subject.
2. Our class (is, are) studying the American colonies.
3. Williamsburg (was, were) a colonial community.
4. Actors (play, plays) the part of colonists.
5. A blacksmith (pound, pounds) metal at a forge.

B If the subject and verb of a sentence agree, write *C* for correct. If they do not agree, write the sentence, changing the verb to make it agree with the subject.

1. Narrative poems tells stories.
2. Often they are about a nation's heroes.
3. This poem tell of a patriot's courage.
4. Mr. Kuropas always reads this poem aloud to his classes.
5. Every student listen spellbound.
6. Many vivid images comes to life for the students.
7. The hero faces many dangers.
8. He continue for the sake of his countrymen.
9. Such stories creates pride in our country and its heroes.
10. Liberty are the common goal for Americans yesterday and today.

C Add a verb that tells about the present time to complete each sentence. Be sure to use the verb form that agrees with the subject. Write the sentences.

11. The colonial era _____ my favorite part of American history.
12. I _____ many books about the Revolutionary War.
13. If a book is too hard, Dad _____ it to me.
14. The Minutemen _____ very brave to me.
15. Dad and I _____ them fighting the mighty British army.
16. We _____ about each book after we finish it.

Test Preparation

✓ Write the letter of the verb that agrees with the subject in the sentence.

1. Most kids ____ about Ben Franklin.

   A know   C knowing
   B knows   D knos

2. He ____ something of a national treasure.

   A are   C were
   B is   D being

3. History teachers ____ about his political genius.

   A talking   C talker
   B talks   D talk

4. Scientists ____ his inventions and discoveries.

   A praiseing   C praises
   B praise   D praising

5. People ____ Franklin's wise sayings.

   A quotes   C quotable
   B quote   D quoting

6. "A stitch in time ____ nine."

   A saving   C saves
   B save   D saver

7. Those words ____ one famous Franklin quotation.

   A is   C being
   B are   D making

8. His practical advice ____ Americans well.

   A serving   C server
   B serves   D serve

9. The Franklin stove ____ just one of his scientific contributions.

   A be   C are
   B were   D is

10. A high-flying kite ____ us of his electricity experiments.

    A remind   C reminds
    B reminding   D reminder

Review

 Write the subject of each sentence. Then write the verb in ( ) that agrees with this subject.

1. Historical fiction (is, are) make-believe stories based on real events or people.
2. An example of historical fiction (is, are) the novel *Ben and Me*.
3. The main characters (is, are) Ben Franklin and a mouse named Amos.
4. In the novel, Amos (take, takes) credit for Franklin's work.
5. The little mouse (live, lives) in Franklin's wig.
6. Readers (laugh, laughs) while they learn about history.
7. Robert Lawson (is, are) the author of *Ben and Me*.
8. Children of all ages (enjoy, enjoys) this lighthearted book.
9. Our social studies teacher (is, are) reading it to us.
10. We (discuss, discusses) Ben Franklin's real-life accomplishments.

 Add a present tense verb to complete each sentence. Be sure the verb agrees with the subject in number.

11. Thomas Jefferson's home _____ on a mountaintop in Virginia.
12. Monticello _____ many visitors each year.
13. Its ingenious architecture _____ Jefferson's love of classical design.
14. Its many gardens _____ his devotion to agriculture and science.
15. Many original inventions by Jefferson _____ displayed in the house.
16. Visitors _____ Jefferson's genius as they tour the home and grounds.

Organization

When **organizing** your writing about an event, use sequence words to make it clear when each action occurred. Some sequence words are *at first, next, then, now,* and *finally.*

Choose a sequence word or phrase from the box to begin each sentence. Write the sentences as a paragraph.

after rising	in the afternoon
finally	at daybreak
following this record keeping	then

Thomas Jefferson rose from his bed.

He measured and recorded the temperature and other weather data.

He started a fire to warm his room and dressed for the day.

This man of letters sat down at his writing table and wrote letters.

The master of Monticello inspected his vegetable and fruit gardens.

Jefferson mounted his horse and toured his five farms for the rest of the day.

Write your own paragraph about something you have accomplished. Use sequence words to show the order of events.

Writing for Tests

> **Prompt**   In an interview, a person answers questions about himself or herself. "Interview" a famous person from history whom you have read about. Write questions and answers that are based on your reading. Try to make this person "come alive" for your audience.

Question focuses on circumstances under which Declaration was written.

Champion of Freedom: Thomas Jefferson Speaks

Q: Why did you write the Declaration of Independence?

A: I represented my colony of Virginia in the Continental Congress. The colonies were going to war with Britain for their independence. I was asked to write an explanation of our reasons for fighting.

Q: Did you write the Declaration all yourself?

Sequence words clarify order of events.

A: Yes, I felt strongly about our right to liberty. Within a few days, I had a draft. Next, I showed it to Benjamin Franklin and John Adams, and they helped improve it. Then Congress debated about it and insisted on a few changes.

Question focuses on how person thought and felt.

Q: How did you feel about that?

Details communicate emotions of author.

A: It was agony. These were my deepest beliefs on paper. However, I knew all the colonies had to agree on the words. Congress struck out the paragraph condemning slavery. I hated that. Even though I owned slaves, I knew slavery was evil and needed to end.

Past, Present, and Future Tenses

The **tense** of a verb shows when something happens. Verbs in the **present tense** show action that happens now. Most present tense singular verbs end with *-s* or *-es*. Most present tense plural verbs do not end with *-s* or *-es*.

The king <u>enters</u> the hall. His subjects <u>bow</u>.

Verbs in the **past tense** show action that has already happened. Most verbs in the past tense end in *-ed*.

Long ago, a fairy <u>enchanted</u> the princess.

Verbs in the **future tense** show action that will happen. Add *will* (or *shall*) to most verbs to show the future tense.

She <u>will sleep</u> now.

- Some regular verbs change spelling when *-ed* is added. For verbs ending in *e*, drop the *e* and add *-ed*: *liked, loved.* For verbs ending in a consonant and *y*, change the *y* to *i*, and add *-ed*: *hurried, carried.*

- For most one-syllable verbs that end in one vowel followed by one consonant, double the consonant and add *-ed: stopped, napped.*

- Irregular verbs change spelling to form the past tense: *are/were, become/became, bring/brought, eat/ate, fly/flew, give/gave, have/had, is/was, meet/met, sing/sang, take/took, tell/told, write/wrote.*

A Identify the tense of each verb. Write *present, past,* or *future.*

1. wants
2. will award
3. competed
4. is
5. received
6. calls
7. will ring
8. tried

B Copy the table. Complete it by filling in the missing tenses of verbs.

Present	Past	Future
1. You plan.	You ____.	You ____.
2. He ____.	He ate.	He ____.
3. They marry.	They ____.	They ____.
4. It flies.	It ____.	It ____.
5. She hopes.	She ____.	She ____.
6. We ____.	We smiled.	We ____.
7. I give.	I ____.	I ____.

C In each item, one sentence uses the wrong verb tense. Rewrite that sentence, correcting the verb.

8. I will be a pilot someday. I will set all kinds of records for speed. I travel the world.

9. Fairy tales were passed down orally for centuries. Grandparents and parents told them to their children. The Brothers Grimm write down these tales in the 1800s.

10. Tales usually involve kings, queens, princes, and princesses. A young person seeks his or her fortune. A terrible problem was solved. All is well at the end.

11. Bruce will fly to Dallas this summer. He visited his aunt, uncle, and cousins. They will take him with them to a game in Houston.

12. Penny writes stories. She illustrated them too. She reads them to groups of young children.

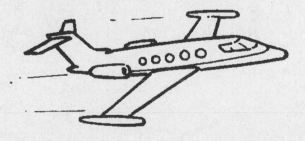

Test Preparation

✓ Write the letter of the verb that correctly completes the sentence.

1. Our class ___ studying great inventors now.

   A is   **C** am
   B was   **D** will be

2. Alexander Graham Bell ___ the telephone in 1875.

   A invent   **C** invented
   B invents   **D** will invent

3. Today, the first phones ___ odd to us.

   A looked   **C** looks
   B look   **D** will look

4. Some day, cell phones ___ old fashioned too.

   A seem   **C** seemed
   B seems   **D** will seem

5. The computer ___ an important invention of the twentieth century.

   A is   **C** am
   B was   **D** will be

6. Because of computers, we ___ our time the Age of Information.

   A call   **C** called
   B calls   **D** will call

7. In the 1990s, the Internet ___ us access to a world of information.

   A give   **C** gave
   B gives   **D** will give

8. The future ___ many more inventions.

   A bring   **C** brang
   B brings   **D** will bring

Review

✔ Identify the tense of each underlined verb. Write *past, present,* or *future.*

1. Our middle school <u>has</u> a drama club.
2. Last year, thirty students <u>joined</u> the club.
3. Members <u>vote</u> on a play to perform.
4. This year, the club <u>will perform</u> a musical.
5. The club <u>meets</u> every Thursday.
6. Soon we <u>will hold</u> tryouts for parts.
7. Many students <u>try</u> out.
8. I <u>want</u> a singing part in the musical.
9. I <u>watched</u> musicals on TV.
10. I <u>sang</u> along with them for practice.

✔ Rewrite each sentence twice. First, change the underlined verb to past tense. Then change it to future tense.

11. I <u>fly</u> in a jet.
12. Our family <u>vacations</u> far from home.
13. A plane <u>reduces</u> our travel time.
14. It <u>takes</u> two days to drive to the coast.
15. The jet <u>carries</u> us there in six hours.
16. It <u>stops</u> twice on the way.
17. Sometimes the altitude change <u>bothers</u> my ears.
18. I <u>yawn</u> to equalize the pressure in my ears.
19. I <u>walk</u> around every hour.
20. The trip <u>is</u> over surprisingly fast.

Use Powerful Verbs

A skit or play focuses on action. Use **powerful verbs** in stage directions so actors know exactly how to move or speak. Use vivid verbs in dialogue to make actors' words convincing.

 Read each pair of stage directions. Write the letter of the stage direction that best explains what actors should do.

1. A *QUEEN walks left to right, looks out window.*

   B *QUEEN strides left to right, stares out window sadly.*

2. A *KING dashes up stairs, barks order over his shoulder.*

   B *KING runs up stairs, gives order over his shoulder.*

3. A *PRINCESS brushes hair slowly, looks in mirror.*

   B *PRINCESS strokes hair gently with brush, gazes longingly in mirror.*

4. A *JESTER laughs loudly and makes noise.*

   B *JESTER guffaws and stamps his foot.*

 For each pair of verbs in ( ), write the verb that makes the stage direction more vivid.

(5) PRINCE GAWKY (gets up, leaps) from his chair. **(6)** He (trips, falls) over the hassock and (goes, rolls) across the floor. **(7)** He (hauls, pulls) himself up using a table for support. **(8)** The table tips over, and dishes (crash, drop) to the floor. **(9)** They (break, smash) into bits. **(10)** PRINCE GAWKY (dashes, runs) up the stairs but trips over a runner and (falls, topples) again.

 Write a stage direction that describes the actions of an angry king.

Skit

A **skit** is a short play. The plot of a skit is told through **dialogue**—words characters speak. The speaker's name appears before the words. **Stage directions** describe the scene or tell actors how to move.

Bird Catchers

Setting:	*Backyard. Rope, box, and stick lie on ground.*
	Alice and Tom sit on steps, looking frustrated.
ALICE:	We've been trying all morning.
TOM:	We'll never catch a bird! They're too quick.
	(Alice and Tom hang their heads and slump, lost in thought. Enter Mom.)
MOM:	Why so glum? Did you lose something?
ALICE:	We want a pet bird, but we can't catch one.
TOM:	We tried sneaking up on them.
ALICE:	They won't hop in our trap. It's impossible!
MOM:	Hmmm. Why do you want to have a wild bird for a pet? You can't snuggle or pet it.
TOM:	We want to see them up close. They're cool!
MOM:	Yes, they are cool, but they need to be free. I have an idea.
	(All leave stage. They re-enter carrying an apple on a string, covered with peanut butter and birdseed. They tie it onto a bush.)
TOM:	We can watch the birds through the window.
ALICE:	They'll be close, but they'll be free.

Stage directions make clear what actors should do.

Dialogue presents the characters' problem.

Specific verbs make dialogue clear.

Principal Parts of Regular Verbs

A verb's tenses are made from four basic forms. These basic forms are called the verb's **principal parts**.

Present	Present Participle	Past	Past Participle
stop	*(is, are)* stopping	stopped	*(has, have, had)* stopped
ask	*(is, are)* asking	asked	*(has, have, had)* asked

A **regular verb** forms its past and past participle by adding *-ed* to the present form.

- The present and the past form can be used by themselves as verbs.
- The present participle and the past participle are always used with a helping verb.

A Write *present, present participle, past,* or *past participle* to identify which principal part the underlined verb is.

1. Genius sometimes <u>slows</u> productivity.
2. Leonardo da Vinci <u>possessed</u> great genius.
3. Yolanda <u>borrowed</u> a biography of Leonardo.
4. It <u>describes</u> his many unfinished projects.
5. Leonardo <u>invented</u> many machines.
6. Only the drawings <u>have survived</u>.
7. His inventions <u>are functioning</u> perfectly well.
8. We <u>have constructed</u> models from his drawings.
9. A few of his magnificent paintings <u>have lasted</u>.
10. The *Mona Lisa* <u>is attracting</u> more crowds now than ever.

B Write the form of the underlined verb indicated in ( ).

1. Throughout the ages, inventors <u>move</u> civilization forward. (past participle)

2. They always <u>imagine</u> ways to make life easier or better. (present participle)

3. Leonardo da Vinci <u>accomplish</u> much as an inventor and an artist. (past)

4. Later inventors <u>study</u> his ideas. (past)

5. Today we still <u>tap</u> his ideas to improve our world. (present participle)

6. Da Vinci's careful diagrams <u>provide</u> a basis for later successes. (past participle)

7. Most people <u>admire</u> the brilliance of da Vinci's work. (present)

8. They <u>wonder</u> how he thought of so many different ideas. (present)

C Write each sentence using the past participle form of the verb in ( ). Decide whether *has* or *have* is needed.

9. I (purchase) a book about Leonardo da Vinci.

10. Hannah (try) to understand his paintings for years.

11. She (describe) his *Mona Lisa* to me several times.

12. Now I (view) it for myself.

13. I see why viewers (puzzle) over it for centuries.

14. Experts (preserve) this masterpiece carefully.

15. Da Vinci's *Last Supper* (weather) the centuries badly.

16. The paint (dry) and cracked.

17. Its broad outlines and some details (survive).

18. The genius of da Vinci (inspire) art lovers for more than five hundred years.

Test Preparation

✓ Write the letter of the principal part used to form the underlined verb in each sentence.

1. Italians <u>valued</u> great artists of the Renaissance.

   A present
   B present participle
   C past
   D past participle

2. They <u>supported</u> artists with their patronage.

   A present
   B present participle
   C past
   D past participle

3. Patronage <u>means</u> "support from a wealthy sponsor."

   A present
   B present participle
   C past
   D past participle

4. Notebooks <u>contained</u> many sketches for paintings.

   A present
   B present participle
   C past
   D past participle

5. People <u>have remarked</u> about the curious writing.

   A present
   B present participle
   C past
   D past participle

6. Da Vinci <u>recorded</u> his ideas in code.

   A present
   B present participle
   C past
   D past participle

Review

Write *present, present participle, past,* or *past participle* to identify which principal part the underlined verb is.

1. A sculptor <u>shapes</u> stone, clay, or metal.

2. A painter <u>uses</u> oils or watercolors.

3. I <u>have tried</u> both these kinds of art.

4. Now I <u>am painting</u> a portrait.

5. During his lifetime, people <u>hailed</u> da Vinci as a genius.

6. Today, many of his works <u>have disappeared</u>.

7. He <u>filled</u> thousands of pages with notes, drawings, and plans.

8. Some of his notebooks <u>have survived</u> to the present.

9. They <u>show</u> a genius fascinated by science, math, and human anatomy.

10. Da Vinci <u>painted</u> to earn a living, but many other interests called him.

Write the sentence using the form of the underlined verb indicated in ( ).

11. In the 1400s and 1500s, most artists <u>paint</u> religious subjects. (past)

12. Today, artists <u>possess</u> much more freedom. (present)

13. Some of them even <u>use</u> computers. (present participle)

14. Our class <u>visit</u> the art museum. (past participle)

15. Tana <u>look</u> at modern paintings. (present participle)

16. Their meaning <u>worry</u> her. (present participle)

17. The artists <u>shun</u> any imitation of reality. (past participle)

18. Tana <u>like</u> the energy and color of the paintings. (present)

Stick to the Topic

An essay explores a single topic. All the paragraphs and supporting ideas in an essay must **stick to the topic**. No matter how interesting they seem, irrelevant details weaken the essay by distracting readers from its purpose.

 Read each main idea sentence for an essay and the supporting details that follow it. Write the letters of any details that DO NOT stick to the topic.

1. Inventors are practical and resourceful people.
   - **A** The telephone and computer are important inventions.
   - **B** Inventors come up with new devices to solve problems.
   - **C** Many times, inventions are the result of an immediate, everyday need.
   - **D** Inventors try many different ideas; they gather all kinds of resources to help them.

2. Leonardo da Vinci thought like a scientist.
   - **A** His notebooks contain thousands of scientific drawings and careful observations.
   - **B** He dissected cadavers to understand human anatomy so he could draw the human form.
   - **C** As an engineer, he created many original machines.
   - **D** He worked for many famous men of his time.

 Write three sentences to support the main idea sentence below. Be sure your details stick to the topic.

The automobile was an invention that revolutionized transportation in the world.

Question/Answer Essay

You may be asked to write an essay to answer a question. The question is the focus of the essay. In the introduction, write a sentence that answers the question and briefly explains your choice. In the body of the essay, develop your answer with supporting details. Summarize your point in the conclusion.

Title poses the question to be answered.

Introduction answers question and gives writer's point of view.

Details and examples support main idea.

Conclusion summarizes main idea and provides an insight.

What Made Leonardo a Great Inventor?

The quality in Leonardo da Vinci most responsible for making him a success was his ability to ask good questions and then find the answers. Because an inventor must understand how things work, questions frame the way he or she explores the what, why, and how of the world.

For example, Leonardo da Vinci wondered, "How do birds fly?" and "What would make it possible for people to fly?" These questions spurred Leonardo to observe birds in flight. He analyzed their muscles and wing structure. He knew that he must think about flying in a new way. How could the structure of a bird's body be imitated and used by humans? He plotted, sketched, and planned ways to imitate the wings of birds.

By answering such questions, Leonardo moved beyond curiosity and closer to discovery. He and his questions were ahead of his time. Although it would take another 400 years before humans succeeded in conquering the air with wings, Leonardo was the first to make a plan for a flying machine.

Principal Parts of Irregular Verbs

Usually you add *-ed* to a verb to show past tense. **Irregular verbs** do not follow this rule. Instead of having *-ed* forms to show past tense, irregular verbs usually change to other words.

Present	Present Participle (*is, are*)	Past	Past Participle (*has, have, had*)
become	becoming	became	become
begin	beginning	began	begun
buy	buying	bought	bought
do	doing	did	done
freeze	freezing	froze	frozen
go	going	went	gone
is/are	being	was/were	been
know	knowing	knew	known
make	making	made	made
see	seeing	saw	seen
think	thinking	thought	thought
write	writing	wrote	written

A Identify which principal part the underlined verb is. Write *present*, *present participle*, *past*, or *past participle*.

1. We <u>are seeing</u> enormous models of *T rex*.
2. <u>Have</u> you <u>thought</u> about these fierce animals?
3. The models <u>freeze</u> them in time and space.
4. Suddenly, the models <u>began</u> moving!
5. My cousins <u>buy</u> a small model.
6. They <u>have become</u> dinosaur fans.

B Write the verb in ( ) that correctly completes each sentence.

1. Our class (has went, went) to a museum of natural history.

2. We (saw, seen) models of many kinds of dinosaurs.

3. Everyone (has became, became) interested in these giant animals.

4. Now we (are doing, are done) projects about dinosaurs.

5. Kyle (has wrote, is writing) a report on velociraptors.

6. Heather (has began, has begun) a book about dinosaurs.

7. She (bought, buyed) it at the museum.

8. Always Jorges (has been, has be) a dinosaur nut.

9. He (is made, is making) a model of a triceratops.

10. I now (known, know) much more about dinosaurs.

11. The models (freeze, frozen) the images of dinosaurs in your mind.

12. I (thought, has thought) dinosaurs were fascinating, and I was right.

C Complete each sentence using the form of the underlined verb in ( ). Write the sentences.

13. Danielle go to the hobby store frequently. (present)

14. She always buy a model of some kind. (present participle)

15. Last week she see a *Tyrannosaurus rex* model. (past)

16. She think it was very cool. (past)

17. Ever since, Danielle is sure she wanted it. (past participle)

18. Now she buy it and begin to put it together. (past participle, present participle)

19. She do many other models. (past participle)

20. Danielle become quite an expert model maker. (present participle)

Test Preparation

✔ Write the letter of the verb that completes each sentence.

1. Sally _____ several children's books.

   A has wrote
   B is wrote
   C has written
   D has writing

2. I _____ all her books.

   A is bought
   B have buyed
   C buyed
   D have bought

3. Now she _____ a book about ancient life forms.

   A written
   B is writing
   C has wrote
   D is written

4. These life forms _____ extinct today.

   A be   **C** are
   B is being   **D** is

5. Some specimens _____ in ice.

   A is froze
   B frozen
   C froze
   D have freezing

6. Others _____ fossils.

   A has became
   B becomed
   C is became
   D have become

7. Scientists _____ careful as they study these remains.

   A are being   **C** has been
   B be   **D** been

8. Everyone _____ to Sally's book signing.

   A has went
   B is going
   C gone
   D be going

Review

 Write *present, present participle, past,* or *past participle* to identify which principal part the underlined verb is.

1. Some artists <u>make</u> models of animals for museums.
2. As they work, they <u>are seeing</u> what the finished model will look like.
3. They <u>know</u> what the animal's skeleton is like.
4. Before they start, they <u>have thought</u> about each step.
5. Their task <u>is</u> no less than to freeze the animal in time and space.
6. Scientists <u>have written</u> their beliefs about the animal.
7. <u>Are</u> you <u>going</u> to the dinosaur exhibit?
8. We <u>were</u> there last week.
9. We <u>thought</u> long and hard about the exhibit.
10. What those artists <u>did</u> is truly miraculous.

 Write the sentence using the form of the underlined verb indicated in ( ).

11. Tess <u>become</u> an expert on dinosaurs. (present participle)
12. A year ago, she <u>know</u> very little about them. (past)
13. Then she <u>become</u> a fan of the ancient creatures. (past)
14. She <u>make</u> every effort to learn about them. (past)
15. Since then, she <u>write</u> many reports on dinosaurs. (past participle)
16. She also <u>make</u> many drawings of them. (past participle)
17. Tess even <u>think</u> about a class at the university. (present participle)
18. I <u>know</u> few people as determined as Tess. (past participle)

What Makes a Paragraph?

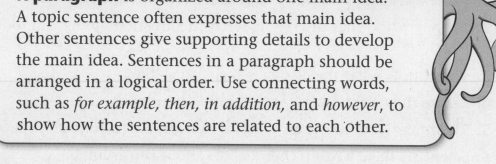

A **paragraph** is organized around one main idea. A topic sentence often expresses that main idea. Other sentences give supporting details to develop the main idea. Sentences in a paragraph should be arranged in a logical order. Use connecting words, such as *for example, then, in addition,* and *however,* to show how the sentences are related to each other.

Read the sentences. Decide on a logical order for them. Write the numbers for the sentences in the order you would place them in a paragraph. Circle the number of the topic sentence.

1. A small, exact model of the dinosaur is created in clay.
2. She creates a hard mold around the clay dinosaur shape.
3. The concrete dinosaur is held in place by a metal skeleton and stone foundation.
4. The sculptor uses the small model as a guide to make a life-size clay model.
5. Building a life-size model of a dinosaur is a monumental task.
6. This hollow mold is used to create a concrete casting of the dinosaur.

Write a paragraph using the sentences from the first exercise. Add connecting words, such as *first, then, next,* and *so on,* to the detail sentences to make them fit together smoothly. End the paragraph with a concluding sentence.

Feature Story

A **feature story** in a newspaper tells about an interesting event or person. Its purpose is to inform and entertain. A feature story needs a catchy lead. Its paragraphs should be logically developed and include lively details.

The feature story that follows was published in a newspaper in 1871.

Dinosaurs Disappear—Again

Lead grabs attention with a surprising detail.

A sculptor's dream of a museum filled with dinosaurs was broken and buried last night—literally! Life-size models of dinosaurs by British sculptor Waterhouse Hawkins were bashed to pieces.

Paragraph tells about sculptor's unusual work.

Hawkins, who came to the United States in 1868, is famous for his giant models of "terrible lizards." Working from bones of the extinct beasts, Hawkins had constructed life-size statues of dinosaurs such as the 30-foot-long iguanodon.

The public was eagerly awaiting the unveiling at the opening of a special museum in New York. That hope was destroyed when unknown vandals broke into Hawkins's studio last night.

Quote by sculptor adds interest and captures mood of outrage.

The enraged sculptor said, "This is awful! These creations cannot be replaced. How could anyone destroy them?"

Final sentence concludes story and gives reader something to think about.

Even the pieces of the statues are missing. Like the dinosaurs they represented, the statues have disappeared from the face of the Earth.

Troublesome Verbs

Some pairs of verbs are confusing because they have similar meanings or because they look alike.

Word	Meaning	Present	Past	Past Participle
lay	put, place	lay	laid	(*has, have, had*) laid
lie	rest, recline	lie	lay	(*has, have, had*) lain
set	put something somewhere	set	set	(*has, have, had*) set
sit	sit down	sit	sat	(*has, have, had*) sat
let	allow	let	let	(*has, have, had*) let
leave	go away	leave	left	(*has, have, had*) left

A Write the form of the underlined verb indicated in ( ).

1. I <u>sit</u> in the front row at the gospel and blues convention. (past)

2. Someone had <u>set</u> a program on every seat. (past participle)

3. A crew had <u>lay</u> a platform stage on the floor. (past participle)

4. The lead singer had <u>lie</u> down for a short nap. (past participle)

5. If you <u>leave</u> your seat, you lost it. (past)

6. Ushers <u>let</u> no one in after the performance started. (past)

7. A tall woman in a hat had <u>sit</u> in front of me. (past participle)

8. If she had <u>set</u> that hat aside, I would have been able to see better. (past participle)

9. If someone had <u>left</u>, I could have moved. (past participle)

10. Finally, the woman <u>lay</u> her hat on her lap. (past)

B Write the verb that correctly completes the sentence. Use context to help you decide which verb is needed.

1. Bree (sat, set) with her mom and dad.
2. The baby (lay, laid) in the stroller sleeping.
3. Bree (lay, laid) her program on her lap.
4. Dad had (sat, set) the picnic basket on the ground.
5. Mom had (laid, lain) down on the picnic blanket for a quick nap.
6. Bree was glad her parents had (left, let) her stay up for the concert.
7. The bandleader (left, let) the podium.
8. The musicians stood to take a bow and then (sat, set) down again.
9. Since no one had (left, let), the band played an encore.
10. The audience wouldn't (leave, let) them stop playing.
11. Because we (sat, set) on the ground for two hours, it was hard to get up.
12. We should not have (left, let) our lawn chairs at home.

C Choose the form of *lie* or *lay* indicated in ( ). Use the chart to help you. Write the sentence.

13. Mom ＿＿＿ a hand on my forehead. (past)
14. I had ＿＿＿ in bed all morning with a fever. (past participle)
15. She said, " ＿＿＿ those books and magazines on the floor." (present)
16. I asked, "Can I listen to CDs while I ＿＿＿ here?" (present)
17. This blues CD has ＿＿＿ on the shelf for years. (past participle)
18. Soon Mom ＿＿＿ down with me to listen. (past)

Test Preparation

✓ Write the letter of the verb that correctly completes each sentence.

1. Ona usually ___ on the couch to watch TV.

   A laid   C lain
   B lies   D lays

2. I usually ___ in this chair.

   A sit   C set
   B setted   D set

3. Grandpa has ___ for the airport.

   A leave   C left
   B let   D leaved

4. The jeweler has ___ three rings on the counter.

   A sit   C sat
   B set   D sitted

5. The singer has ___ her music on the piano.

   A lie   C laid
   B lay   D lain

6. She has not ___ herself become nervous about performing.

   A leave   C left
   B let   D letted

7. Philip ___ on a lounge chair, fast asleep.

   A lie   C lay
   B laid   D lain

8. ___ the first two rows empty.

   A Leave   C Left
   B Let   D Leaved

9. Who ___ on my hat?

   A sit   C sitted
   B set   D sat

10. The dogs ___ in the sun every afternoon.

   A lied   C laid
   B lie   D lain

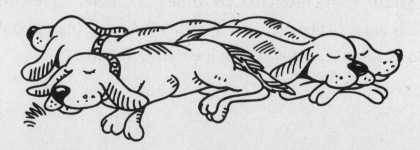

Review

 Complete the chart. Write the missing verb tenses for each verb.

Present	Past	Past Participle
1. ____	left	____
2. let	____	____
3. lay	____	____
4. ____	____	have lain
5. ____	____	have sat
6. ____	set	____

Write the verb that correctly completes the sentence.

7. Few people have (laid, lain) on a bed of nails.

8. Today I will (set, sit) with you.

9. (Set, Sit) your boots on the mat.

10. The piano teacher (sat, set) beside the youngest student.

11. Vince had (laid, lain) a bouquet on a chair.

12. Ginny (sat, set) the bouquet in a vase of water.

13. She asked her teacher, "Will you (leave, let) me play another piece?"

14. Most of the audience had (left, let) the auditorium.

15. Before beginning to play, she (lay, laid) her hands in her lap.

16. This step (left, let) her focus on the piece she would play.

17. A litter of instrument cases (lay, laid) on the practice room floor.

18. The audience had (sat, set) spellbound as she played.

19. I had (sat, set) my purse on the floor under my chair.

20. I (let, left) it there while I stood and applauded.

 **WRITER'S CRAFT**

Use Specific Words

In a description, use **specific words** to help your reader see what you are describing. For example, instead of *art*, use *painting* or *sculpture*. Instead of *good*, use *skillful* or *honorable*.

 Read the general phrase and the specific phrase that is substituted on the right. Write another phrase that uses specific words to create a vivid picture.

General	Specific
1. a good father	a strict but affectionate father
2. enjoyable music	a peppy salsa song
3. a nice time	an exciting afternoon at the water park
4. awesome talent	clear Irish tenor
5. pretty scenery	towering peaks in a purple haze
6. a scared pup	a tiny brown poodle cowering under a chair
7. interesting information	an exciting, inspiring speech
8. a boring movie	a real snooze fest of a film
9. a helpful person	a friendly, knowledgeable salesclerk
10. a new food	crisp rice noodles with pan-fried shrimp

 Write a description of a person who impresses you. Include specific nouns and vivid adjectives.

Description

A **description** helps readers visualize a place, person, or thing. It creates a word picture using vivid sense words and images. A description may use strong details to create a feeling, such as happiness or fear. It can be organized by space order (for example, top to bottom) or by senses (for example, smell, sight, taste).

Strong title and opening set this piece in motion.

Description is ordered by type of instrument in band.

Vivid images create upbeat, lively mood.

A Little Marching Music, Maestro

There's nothing like a John Philip Sousa march to fill a room with energy. No one can frown or slump while listening to a marching band play "The Stars and Stripes Forever." The sound sets my toes tapping and gives me a "can-do" attitude.

Snare drums beat a commanding rhythm. *Rat-a-tat tat. Rat-a-tat-tat.* I feel the thump of the bass drum from head to toe. *Boom, boom, boom.* The brass joins in with a powerful melody. Then suddenly a flute rises above the concert of sound. *Dee-dee-dee-dee-dee-dee.*

If I close my eyes, I can see Sousa leading his marching band on parade. The plumes on the players' hats bob, and the brass on the shoulders of their uniforms sparkles. I feel like marching around the room!

My friends say rap and rock are the best kinds of music, but give me a Sousa march any day!

Prepositions and Prepositional Phrases

A **preposition** begins a group of words called a **prepositional phrase.** The noun or pronoun that follows the preposition is called the **object of the preposition.** Prepositional phrases provide details about the rest of the sentence.

Animation is created <u>from</u> careful drawings.
(preposition)

Animation is created <u>from careful drawings</u>.
(prepositional phrase)

Animation is created from careful <u>drawings</u>.
(object of the preposition)

Common Prepositions

about	around	by	into	over	until
above	at	down	near	through	up
across	before	for	of	to	with
after	below	from	on	toward	
against	between	in	onto	under	

A Write the prepositional phrase in each sentence. Circle the preposition.

1. The first animated cartoons were made by Walt Disney.
2. Disney created Mickey Mouse in 1928.
3. This film used sound for the first time.
4. Viewers loved the little mouse with the silly grin.
5. Mickey's looks changed over time.
6. Today he is beloved around the world.
7. Many millions of people visit Disney World and Disneyland.
8. There you can see Mickey strolling across the grounds.

B Write the prepositional phrase in each sentence. Write *P* above the preposition. Write *O* above the object of the preposition.

1. Two of my favorite animated films are *Shrek* and *The Incredibles*.

2. The ogre Shrek is kind at heart.

3. Shrek's swamp is crowded with annoying fairy-tale characters.

4. They are there against their will.

5. Lord Farquaad sends Shrek to a far-off castle.

6. The beautiful Princess Fiona must be rescued from a fire-breathing dragon.

7. Fiona has a secret, however, that causes more trouble for Shrek.

8. The characters seem real and lovable to me.

9. They made me care about them.

10. Which character in the movie is your favorite?

C Add a prepositional phrase of your own to complete each sentence. Write the sentence.

11. Computers have made moviemaking simpler _____ .

12. Many special effects are created _____ .

13. Animators are artists _____ .

14. Once, they had to make thousands of drawings _____ .

15. Computers have removed much of the drudgery _____ .

16. Computer programs will color and add texture _____ .

17. The characters move and speak _____ .

18. Computer animation will become even more amazing _____ .

Test Preparation

Write the letter of the preposition that correctly completes each sentence in the paragraph.

(1) Mr. Incredible was one ____ the greatest superheroes. (2) Now he's just a civilian ____ a job. (3) He, his wife, and three kids live ____ the suburbs. (4) Mr. Incredible has become an insurance adjuster ____ the name of Bob Paar. (5) He once fought evil ____ a daily basis. (6) Now he fights ____ an expanding waistline. (7) ____ many boring days, he longs for real action. (8) Then he is summoned mysteriously ____ a remote island. (9) What top-secret assignment will once more turn him ____ Mr. Incredible? (10) ____ the animated film *The Incredibles*, you will find out.

1. A for	**C** of	**6. A** against	**C** under
B with	**D** at	**B** below	**D** to
2. A with	**C** against	**7. A** Until	**C** Toward
B from	**D** by	**B** Near	**D** After
3. A until	**C** in	**8. A** down	**C** by
B before	**D** under	**B** to	**D** under
4. A against	**C** across	**9. A** from	**C** into
B through	**D** by	**B** around	**D** at
5. A until	**C** about	**10. A** In	**C** To
B on	**D** with	**B** About	**D** Above

Review

 Write *P* if the underlined word is a preposition. Write *O* if it is the object of the preposition.

1. Have you ever made a flip book <u>for</u> fun?
2. A flip book consists of a <u>series</u> of hand-drawn pictures.
3. Each picture places the figure <u>in</u> a slightly different place.
4. You can flip <u>through</u> the pictures quickly.
5. The figure apparently moves from one <u>place</u> to another.
6. This is a crude sort <u>of</u> animation.
7. Early cartoons were all hand-drawn <u>by</u> skillful artists.
8. It took hundreds of drawings to move a character <u>across</u> the screen.
9. Each one was carefully transferred onto <u>celluloid</u>.
10. These artists came amazingly close to <u>perfection</u>.

 Write each prepositional phrase. The number in ( ) tells how many prepositional phrases are in that sentence.

11. For years the name Disney was identified with animation. (2)
12. Walt Disney was a pioneer in the field of animated movies. (2)
13. Mickey Mouse first appeared on the screen in 1928 with the premiere of *Steamboat Willie*. (4)
14. The world would soon fall in love with the little mouse. (2)
15. The field of animation has grown and changed tremendously over time. (2)
16. The role of computers in animation has expanded greatly in recent years. (3)
17. Although Walt Disney has died, his name continues in the films still produced by his company. (2)
18. The animated films made by other companies have competed successfully with Disney's films. (2)

Parallelism

If a sentence has two or more parts that are alike, those parts should have the same form or pattern. **Parallel structure** refers to the pattern, or organization, of similar sentence parts, such as verbs, nouns, and prepositional phrases.

 Write the letter of the parallel sentence in each pair.

1. A I love drawing, painting, and to sculpt.
 B I love drawing, painting, and sculpting.

2. A I hope to become an artist, a cartoonist, or an animator.
 B I hope to become an artist, a cartoonist, or make animated films.

3. A Computer animation is used to create special effects, short cartoons, and make movies that are animated.
 B Computer animation is used to create special effects, short cartoons, and animated movies.

4. A Computers create animated cartoons quickly, efficiently, and with precision.
 B Computers create animated cartoons quickly, efficiently, and precisely.

 Rewrite the sentences in this paragraph to make them parallel.

   Walt put down his pen, looked at the drawing, and sighing with satisfaction. The little mouse looked perky, friendly, and like a character you could love. Soon the animator and his little mouse would gain fame, a bundle of money, and affection around the world.

Writing for Tests

Prompt   Think about an <u>older animated film</u> and a <u>recent animated film</u> you can <u>compare</u>. For example, *Snow White and the Seven Dwarfs* is older, and *The Lion King* is newer. <u>Explain to your class</u> ways they are alike and different. Use <u>parallel structure</u> to present your ideas.

Topic sentence sets up the essay.

Parallel structure is used to present three characteristics.

Transitions show likenesses and differences.

Pinocchio and Finding Nemo

Although they were created in different centuries, Pinocchio and Finding Nemo are animated films with much in common. Both films were animated so skillfully that you forget that you are looking at drawings. The artistry of the animators results in characters, action, and images that captivate viewers.

However, these films are from different eras, and the technology used to produce each movie is quite different. Because it was made before computers, Pinocchio required detailed illustrations by artists. Every image that was photographed was drawn and colored by hand. On the other hand, Finding Nemo is a film of the computer age. Computer animation saved its creators thousands of drawings because software could create "in-between" drawings after the originals were done. Computers were used to add color, texture, and light to drawings. Despite the difference in technology, both films are entertaining and artistic.

Subject and Object Pronouns

A **subject pronoun** is used in the subject of a sentence. Singular subject pronouns are *I, you, he, she,* and *it.* Plural subject pronouns are *we, you,* and *they.* When you use a person's name and a pronoun in a compound subject, be sure to use a subject pronoun.

> <u>We</u> invented an imaginary country. <u>It</u> is far away.
> Liz and <u>I</u> planned a trip there.

An **object pronoun** is used in the predicate of a sentence after an action verb or with a preposition, such as *for, at, into, with,* or *to.* Singular object pronouns are *me, you, him, her,* and *it.* Plural object pronouns are *us, you,* and *them.* When you use a person's name and a pronoun in a compound object, be sure to use an object pronoun.

> That story reminds <u>me</u> of <u>him</u>. Leon told <u>them</u>.
> He helped Jenny and <u>me</u>.

A Write *S* if the underlined word is a subject pronoun. Write *O* if the word is an object pronoun.

1. <u>I</u> would like a treehouse.
2. Will you help <u>me</u> with the project?
3. Dad and <u>we</u> can get lumber and nails.
4. Use this rope to lift materials to Dad and <u>him</u>.
5. <u>You</u> and I have done a fine job.
6. They'll climb up the ladder with <u>us</u>.
7. <u>It</u> will make a great clubhouse.
8. Let's invite Danny and <u>her</u> into our club.
9. <u>She</u> and Jamahl brought sandwiches.
10. Lunch in the branches tasted great to <u>them</u>.

B Write the correct pronoun or pronouns in ( ) to complete each sentence.

1. (She, Her) and (I, me) would like to live on another world.

2. Our friends and (we, us) pretend to be shipwrecked on a remote island.

3. The natives have a civilization that is strange to (she, her) and (I, me).

4. Strange deerlike animals give (they, them) milk and meat.

5. The king and queen do not expect their subjects to provide service for (they, them).

6. Instead, (he, him) and (her, she) give gifts to their subjects.

7. Jan and (I, me) become inventors in this world.

8. Our marvelous inventions bring (us, we) many honors.

9. The royal family presents a medal to (her, she) and (I, me).

10. (They, Them) and (us, we) sit down to a royal feast.

C Use each of the phrases below correctly in a sentence. Write the sentence.

11. you and me

12. Louis and her

13. he and I

14. the neighbors and us

15. their relatives and them

16. one storekeeper and we

17. she and her mother

18. Kelly and they

19. George and him

20. he and it

Test Preparation

☑ Write the letter of the pronoun that correctly completes each sentence.

1. Do ____ like unusual foods?

   A them **C** her

   B him **D** you

2. Gina and ____ try foods from many cultures.

   A me **C** them

   B she **D** us

3. Mickey let ____ taste African couscous.

   A her and me

   B she and I

   C her and we

   D us and they

4. ____ is made from wheat and spices.

   A Him **C** It

   B Them **D** Her

5. Paul and ____ tried a spicy Indian curry.

   A her **C** them

   B he **D** me

6. ____ did not try the Chinese wonton soup.

   A They and he

   B Him and us

   C It and her

   D Them and me

7. My family and ____ add unusual things to our food.

   A me **C** I

   B them **D** him

8. Our cousins and ____ ate a delicious salad last night.

   A it **C** them

   B us **D** we

Review

Write *S* if the underlined word is a subject pronoun. Write *O* if the word is an object pronoun.

1. <u>It</u> is helpful to be adaptable.
2. Dad adapts well, so a new situation doesn't bother <u>him</u>.
3. My parents say that thinking "on our feet" is important for <u>us</u>.
4. <u>You</u> and I will have to adapt to change.
5. Going to a new school sounds scary to <u>me</u>.
6. <u>We</u> can help each other adapt.
7. Serena lost her money, and <u>she</u> needed to call her mom after the movie.
8. Lee loaned <u>her</u> a cell phone, so that's how Serena adapted.

Write the correct pronoun or pronouns in ( ) to complete each sentence.

9. Sam and (I, me) took the train by ourselves.
10. (Us, We) had to change from the Red Line to the Blue Line.
11. After we missed our stop, (he, him) and (I, me) didn't know what to do.
12. I asked a man and a woman for help, and (he, him) and (she, her) directed us to the right track.
13. Aunt Doris and Uncle Bob were not worried about (us, we).
14. (They, Them) knew Sam and (I, me) could figure it out.
15. Aunt Doris called Mr. Bales and Ms. Cruz and asked (he, him) and (she, her) to come to dinner.
16. (We, Us) and Uncle Bob made a chili casserole for the guests and (we, us).

Refer to the Text

You may be asked to write an essay about a story you have read. **Refer to the text**—specific people, things, or incidents in the story—to support your ideas.

 Imagine you are writing a letter to a story character. Write the letter of the text that matches each story character.

1. Goldilocks from *Goldilocks and the Three Bears*

2. Jack from *Jack and the Beanstalk*

3. Hansel and Gretel

4. Sleeping Beauty

5. Cinderella

A Trading the cow for beans sounded like a stupid move, but it was actually brilliant. How did you know the beans were magic?

B What I'd really like to know is did you have any dreams while you were asleep all that time? Did you mind missing out on so many years?

C My stepmother makes me do a lot of work around the house too. My little sisters just play. No fair!

D Furthermore, our son's bed must be replaced. Didn't your parents teach you to respect other people's property?

E You two were very clever to outwit that nearsighted witch. How did you get the courage to shove her in the oven?

 Write a note (or an e-mail) to a character in one of your favorite stories. Refer to things that happen in the story.

E-mail

An **e-mail** is an electronic letter (usually a brief, friendly message) sent by computer. Although an e-mail is often informal, you should still use correct grammar, spelling, and punctuation.

This is standard heading information for every e-mail.

Subject: Being Harry Potter's Best Friend

Date: Wednesday, February 25, 2007 11:47 AM

From: Brad Student

To: Ron Weasley

Dear Ron,

Each paragraph has a topic sentence.

You and I have a lot in common. We both like comic books and DO NOT like taking tests. We also have a best friend who is smarter.

References to the story create connection between the sender and receiver.

I don't know about you, but I sometimes get jealous because my best friend Al seems to be able to do everything a little better than I can. I notice that Harry is the best quidditch player. He always seems to figure out the mysteries that go on at Hogwarts. How do you cope with always being "second fiddle"?

On the other hand, your best friend Harry is often in danger. I admire you for being so loyal to him. I think best friends have to stick together, don't you? There's nothing I wouldn't do for my best friend.

Brad Student

Pronouns and Antecedents

A **pronoun** takes the place of a noun or nouns. An **antecedent**, or referent, is the noun or nouns to which the pronoun refers. A pronoun and its antecedent must agree in number and gender.

Before you use a pronoun, ask yourself whether the antecedent is singular or plural. If the antecedent is singular, decide whether it is masculine, feminine, or neuter. Then choose a pronoun that agrees. In the following sentences, the antecedents are underlined once; the pronouns are underlined twice.

When <u>Emily</u> exercises, <u>she</u> stretches <u>muscles and tendons</u>. <u>They</u> are tight and sore.

A Write each sentence. Underline the antecedent once and the pronoun twice.

1. Sam is happy because he can jump and run.
2. Because Janelle enjoys swimming, she swims on the YMCA team.
3. Janelle and Sam are lucky because they have healthy bodies.
4. Some children have cerebral palsy, and it causes problems with body movement and control.
5. These children need therapy to help them move freely.
6. Nolan uses a wheelchair, and a computer allows him to communicate.
7. The computer has an artificial voice, so it produces spoken words.
8. Megan remains cheerful, although therapy can be painful for her.

B Write the antecedent in each item. Then write the pronoun in ( ) that matches the antecedent.

1. Muscles need exercise to give (it, them) proper tone.

2. Muscle tone is important. (It, They) means muscles have normal tension and respond well.

3. Dad gets exercise by playing golf. (He, It) uses his arms and legs while he plays.

4. Mom walks and jogs. Daily exercise has made (her, them) strong and energetic.

5. I like to play soccer and basketball. (They, We) require plenty of physical exertion.

6. All children need plenty of calcium. Dairy products and leafy green vegetables will give (her, them) calcium.

7. Calcium makes the bones strong. (It, They) also helps the body in other ways.

8. Hannah drinks a glass of milk with lunch. (She, It) likes milk with cookies too.

9. Mr. Causy brought a diagram with (him, it) to explain about diet and fitness.

10. A healthy diet does not have to be boring. (It, They) can be delicious, tasty, and colorful.

C Use each noun-pronoun pair to write a sentence or two. Be sure the noun is the antecedent for the pronoun in each pair.

11. muscles, they
12. dietician, she
13. nutrients, them
14. athlete, she
15. handicap, it

Test Preparation

✓ Write the letter of the pronoun that correctly completes each sentence.

1. Watching babies learn to walk is fun. ____ are unsteady on their feet.

   A Them   **C** It
   B They   **D** She

2. Walking requires several skills. For example, ____ takes balance.

   A it   **C** they
   B her   **D** he

3. The legs move you along, but ____ do not work alone.

   A he   **C** they
   B she   **D** you

4. Arms, feet, and torso work together with the legs. All of ____ must be coordinated.

   A it   **C** them
   B they   **D** he

5. Baby Tina has mastered this skill. Now the world has opened up for ____.

   A her   **C** they
   B she   **D** them

6. Jeffrey learned to walk at ten months. ____ also could climb by then.

   A Him   **C** He
   B She   **D** They

7. Adele and Adam are twins, so people expect ____ to do things at the same pace.

   A her   **C** they
   B them   **D** him

8. Adele walked first, but ____ began to talk later than Adam.

   A them   **C** her
   B they   **D** she

Review

✓ Write the antecedent of the underlined pronoun in each sentence or pair of sentences.

1. Nerve cells are unique. <u>They</u> are called neurons.

2. These special cells send and receive messages. <u>They</u> use electricity and chemicals to do this.

3. Kim drew a picture of a neuron. <u>She</u> labeled its parts.

4. An axon is long and slender. <u>It</u> carries the message away from the cell body.

5. Mr. Harris liked the drawing Kim made and gave <u>her</u> an A on it.

6. Your brain contains billions of neurons. <u>It</u> is the "mastermind" of your nervous system.

7. Nerves branch to all parts of your body. The brain controls <u>them</u>.

✓ Write a pronoun to replace each underlined noun or noun phrase.

8. Some nerves connect to muscles. <u>These nerves</u> tell the muscles to contract.

9. Tamara told Ed about the nervous system and drew a simple diagram for <u>Ed</u>.

10. The brain is the main part of this system, but <u>the brain</u> could not run the body without the spinal cord.

11. Then there are the nerves. Millions of <u>nerves</u> branch out of the spinal cord to all parts of the body.

12. While Tamara explained to the class, Ed did demonstrations. For example, <u>Ed</u> showed how a reflex works.

Elaboration

Writing can be undeveloped or unclear if the writer does not **elaborate** his or her ideas. Exact nouns, verbs, and vivid sensory details can make writing fresh and clear.

Before Elaboration	The sun felt good.
After Elaboration	The bright morning sun warmed and cheered us.
Before Elaboration	We took off on the path.
After Elaboration	We began jogging briskly along the soft dirt path that bordered the park.

 Replace the underlined word or phrase with interesting exact details. Write the new sentence.

1. Shelly soon <u>got tired</u>.
2. Adam <u>did not like waiting</u>.
3. His legs are <u>strong</u>.
4. She practiced running <u>a lot</u>.
5. Now she can run <u>well too</u>.
6. This path <u>is long</u>.
7. After their run, they will <u>rest</u>.
8. Running <u>is good exercise</u>.

 Make the paragraph below more interesting by elaborating the ideas.

A crowd sat in the stands. Runners stretched. The wind blew. Clouds were overhead. Timers got their stopwatches ready. The official lifted the starting gun. The big race was about to begin.

Journal Entry

A journal is a place to "think out loud" on paper. In a **journal entry** you can describe what happened during your day, examine your feelings, or explore an idea. Journal writing can help you make discoveries about yourself and the world.

March 6, 2008

Today I read an article about children with cerebral palsy (CP). At first, I felt sorry for these kids. Imagine not being able to walk and run like other kids do! The stretching exercises they must do to help them move are painful. Any physical activity takes longer than normal and is more difficult for them than it is for me. They may also need operations and special medicines.

I wonder if I would be cheerful and strong like these kids are if I had their problems. I tried not talking for thirty minutes today, and it nearly drove me crazy! I think if it was hard for me to communicate, I would say the most important things first—like "thank you" and "I love you."

The more I think about the CP kids, the more I admire them. They work so hard. They endure pain and face the challenge of being different. They will never have the freedom of movement I have. Yet in the pictures in the article they look so happy! They have that "You bet I can handle it" attitude that gets things done.

Writer examines feelings about kids with cerebral palsy.

Details elaborate by giving reasons for feelings.

Writer makes discovery about self through elaboration.

Writer's viewpoint has changed.

Possessive Pronouns

Possessive pronouns show who or what owns, or possesses, something. *My, mine, your, yours, her, hers, his, its, our, ours, their,* and *theirs* are possessive pronouns.

- Use *my, your, her, our,* and *their* before nouns.

  This is <u>my</u> cat. It was <u>her</u> dog. They fed <u>their</u> fish.
- Use *mine, yours, hers, ours,* and *theirs* alone.

  The cat is <u>mine</u>. The dog was <u>hers</u>. The fish are <u>theirs</u>.
- *His* and *its* can be used both before nouns and alone.

  He found <u>his</u> dog. The dog is <u>his</u>.

  The dog hurt <u>its</u> paw. The paw is <u>its</u>.
- Do not use an apostrophe with a possessive pronoun.

A Write the pronoun that correctly completes each sentence.

1. Ants use (theirs, their) antennae for touch and smell.
2. That nest under the tree is (their, theirs).
3. An ant has two stomachs in (its, our) abdomen.
4. One stomach stores food for other ants to share, and another stomach holds (it's, its) own food.
5. The queen is larger than the other ants, and (her, hers) body is an egg factory.
6. All the worker ants are sterile, so the egg-laying task is all (her, hers).
7. A male ant lives apart from the colony and plays (his, theirs) part by mating with the queen.
8. My family and I sometimes get ants in (our, hers) house.
9. The house with purple trim is (my, mine).
10. Don't have (your, theirs) picnic next to an ant colony!

B Replace the underlined words or phrases with possessive pronouns. Rewrite the sentences.

1. Every living thing must adapt to <u>every living thing's</u> surroundings.

2. Plants are even more affected by <u>plants'</u> surroundings than animals are.

3. Grandpa has a cactus garden in Arizona; the largest cactus in the neighborhood is <u>Grandpa's</u>.

4. Because Arizona is a desert, <u>Arizona's</u> climate is hot and dry.

5. Mary and I observed desert plants and animals on <u>Mary's and my</u> vacation.

6. A cactus has few or no leaves, so the desert sun cannot evaporate all <u>the cactus's</u> water.

7. Some desert plants tap water from deep underground with the <u>desert plants'</u> long roots.

8. The guide advised the hikers to take along canteens, but Dorie and Ed forgot <u>Dorie's and Ed's</u>.

C Each sentence contains a possessive pronoun error. Rewrite the sentences, correcting these errors.

9. People can adapt to its environments too.

10. To escape the winter cold, you probably cover their skin with warmer clothes.

11. Humans can live most anywhere because we can change my environment.

12. We have a furnace to warm our house; you probably have one to warm your too.

13. A whale has a thick layer of fat under our skin to keep out the cold.

14. Birds fluff up his feathers to trap air and keep them warm.

15. I wear a hat to keep their head warm.

16. Dan has a new hat. He likes my hat, but he says he likes its better.

Test Preparation

✓ Write the letter of the pronoun that correctly completes each sentence.

1. Amy and I spent ____ afternoon at the zoo.

  A mine   **C** our
  B her   **D** their

2. The sloths hung by ____ toes from branches.

  A their   **C** his
  B theirs   **D** mine

3. A giraffe stretched ____ long neck into tree branches.

  A yours   **C** hers
  B its   **D** their

4. A mother wolf nursed ____ pups.

  A their   **C** hers
  B his   **D** her

5. The cozy den is ____.

  A theirs   **C** our
  B my   **D** their

6. A male lion chose a sunny rock for ____ nap.

  A theirs   **C** his
  B your   **D** hers

7. ____ favorite was the dolphins.

  A Mine   **C** Ours
  B My   **D** Hers

8. Their intelligence is similar to ____.

  A her   **C** my
  B ours   **D** it's

9. ____ adaptations make all the animals unique.

  A Their   **C** His
  B Theirs   **D** It

10. Amy's favorite is the elephant. Which is ____?

  A my   **C** your
  B her   **D** yours

Review

 Write the possessive pronoun that could replace the underlined possessive noun or noun phrase. Use each pronoun only once.

our	his	hers	their	its	her	theirs	ours

1. The hike was <u>Tony and Noor's</u> idea.
2. Did you like <u>Pablo's and my</u> movie?
3. We all know about <u>Zara's</u> birthday.
4. I would listen to <u>Dad's</u> suggestion.
5. Look at <u>the anteater's</u> snout.
6. The picture is <u>Ed's and mine</u>.
7. The prize was <u>Lisa's</u>.
8. The decision was <u>the judges'</u>.

 Write the pronoun that correctly completes each sentence.

9. We have several animals in (our, ours) classroom.
10. Teams take turns giving the animals (its, their) food.
11. A turtle named John rests in (her, his) terrarium.
12. Sally the goldfish floats in (her, its) aquarium.
13. The gerbils Poco and Allegro are (mine, my) favorites.
14. The bags of cardboard tubes are (my, theirs).
15. Gerbils gnaw on things to wear down (his, their) front teeth.
16. Ms. Gorski brought in animals from (her, hers) pet store.
17. The snake she is holding is actually (its, hers).
18. She showed us how the snake had shed (its, ours) skin.
19. Animal Hour in our class is now a favorite of (mine, my).
20. Which wild animal is (theirs, your) favorite?

Mood

The **mood** of a story is the overall feeling it creates for the reader. For example, the mood may be humorous, serious, or suspenseful. Descriptive details, dialogue, and tone help create mood.

Read each passage. Write the word in the box that best describes the mood it creates.

sarcastic   suspenseful   admiring

1. I had to give that housefly credit. It neatly avoided my swatter every time. I know that fly could see in any direction, with its compound eyes. It could fly instantly, without runway or fuel. It could land on the ceiling, out of reach, because its legs were fitted with barbs for hanging on.

2. Of course, the wild animals in this park love it when you leave litter lying around. It is especially amusing when the plastic rings for the six pack of soft drinks are caught on a fox's paw or around a grouse's neck. They can get snared on a tree or bush. Then they can figure out how to free themselves so they won't starve or suffocate. Fun, huh?

3. I held my breath. "All right," I said to myself, "The bear has seen you. Now what?" Should I run for it? Would it attack? What did it want? I stood frozen. It was like one of those awful dreams where you can't move. The bear snuffled noisily at the air and stood on its hind legs, eyeing me carefully.

Write a passage about an animal in which you build a specific mood. Write the mood you hope to create on the first line.

Story About an Animal

A **story** tells about an event or how characters solve a problem. It has a beginning, middle, and end. Dialogue, style, and tone are tools that a writer uses to give a story a certain feeling, or mood. For example, the mood might be humorous or suspenseful.

The Missing Cat

"I can't find Bear!" cried June. Bear was June's half-grown kitten. His name came from his habit of disappearing into boxes and bags and under beds. He would sleep peacefully in the dark while the whole family called and searched. Finally, he would saunter out, yawning blissfully. June decided that the cat was in fact hibernating. These hidey holes were as close to a cave as he could get.

Mom asked, "Have you looked in his favorite caves?"

"Of course, Mom!" June groaned. "Where can he be?"

They sat at the kitchen table and thought. Then they heard a tiny scratching sound. It was coming from one of the drawers! Somehow, Bear had squeezed his way into a kitchen drawer. Now he was happily wedged into the tiniest cave yet.

Finally, June and Mom got Bear unstuck. He walked away, tail in the air, as if he'd just checked out of a deluxe hotel!

Descriptive details create a humorous picture.

Dialogue sounds natural.

Ending creates a memorable, humorous image.

Indefinite and Reflexive Pronouns

Indefinite pronouns may not refer to specific words. They do not always have definite antecedents: Has <u>anyone</u> met the new kid?

Some common indefinite pronouns are listed below:

Singular Indefinite Pronouns

someone, somebody, anyone, anybody, everyone, everybody, something, no one, either, each

Plural Indefinite Pronouns

few, several, both, others, many, all, some

- Use singular verb forms with singular indefinite pronouns and plural verb forms with plural indefinite pronouns: <u>Everyone</u> gets a cookie. <u>Few</u> turn it down.

Reflexive pronouns reflect the action of the verb back on the subject. Reflexive pronouns end in *-self* or *-selves*: We introduced <u>ourselves</u> to her.

Singular Reflexive Pronouns

himself, herself, myself itself, yourself

Plural Reflexive Pronouns

ourselves, yourselves, themselves

A Write the pronoun in each sentence. Write *indefinite* or *reflexive* to identify the kind of pronoun it is. Then write *singular* or *plural* to show its number.

1. Everyone is really thirsty.

2. The boys help themselves to milk.

3. Others want cider or lemonade.

4. Ileana bought herself a soda.

B Write the correct pronoun in ( ) to complete each sentence.

1. (Everybody, Many) wants to have friends.

2. Have you ever thought whether you are a good friend to (yourself, yourselves)?

3. (No one, Others) are often less critical of us than we are.

4. Lin gets mad at (herself, theirself) when she makes mistakes.

5. Then (anyone, several) around her gets blamed.

6. We all need to accept (ourself, ourselves) as imperfect.

7. If I am at ease with (hisself, myself), I accept others as they are.

8. (Few, Somebody) have learned that lesson.

9. (All, Something) tells me it is a lesson that takes time to learn.

10. Time and experience teach us; (both, either) are necessary.

C Choose a pronoun from the box to complete each sentence correctly. Write the sentence. Be sure indefinite pronouns used as subjects agree in number with their verbs.

many	others	themselves	itself

11. ____ of us have a favorite spot to relax.

12. Some like a quiet place where they can be by ____.

13. ____ prefer a place filled with noise and people.

14. Even a mouse will find ____ a quiet place to rest.

Test Preparation

✓ Write the letter of the pronoun that correctly completes each sentence.

1. ____ has sent me a kind note.

   A Many
   B Someone
   C Few
   D Herself

2. It made me feel good about ____.

   A myself
   B hisself
   C theirself
   D ourselves

3. Does ____ know who sent the note?

   A himself
   B yourself
   C herself
   D anybody

4. ____ likes getting a sincere compliment.

   A Many
   B Something
   C Everyone
   D Itself

5. If ____ feel happy, we can be happy too.

   A all
   B theirself
   C no one
   D myself

6. A smile all by ____ is catching.

   A himself
   B yourselves
   C itself
   D herself

7. Test this idea for ____.

   A hisself
   B yourself
   C ourself
   D myself

8. If ____ smiles at you, do you smile back?

   A herself
   B someone
   C both
   D several

Review

 Write the pronoun in each sentence. Write *indefinite* or *reflexive* to identify the kind of pronoun it is. Then write *singular* or *plural* to show its number.

1. No one has told Hap about the surprise farewell party.
2. Janet and TJ had planned the party themselves.
3. Several almost let the secret slip.
4. Everybody will really miss Hap.
5. Hap said, "Put yourself in my place. Moving is stressful."
6. The move will be exciting in itself, though.

 Write the pronoun in ( ) that correctly completes each sentence.

7. The speaker said to the audience, "Let us all give (ourself, ourselves) a hand."
8. He had used (himself, hisself) as an example several times in his speech.
9. He had spoken about how (everybody, both) benefits from laughter.
10. "You can usually make (ourselves, yourself) feel better with a hearty laugh," he insisted.
11. I decided to try it for (ourself, myself).
12. (Few, Something) starts one person giggling.
13. Then (anybody, several) join in.
14. Soon (everyone, others) is laughing helplessly.
15. (Anybody, Many) do feel better after this activity.
16. All should learn to laugh at (themself, themselves).

Good Conclusions

A **good conclusion** should be more than just a restatement of what went before. It could provide an insight, present a twist, or pose a challenge or a question to readers.

 Read the following paragraph. Write the letter of the sentence that is the strongest conclusion for the paragraph. Then explain your choice.

Different sports are popular in different countries around the world. Here in the United States, a popular sport is what we call football. In Europe and South America, the most popular sport is also called football, but it's what we call soccer. In Australia, they play Australian-rules football, which is another game entirely.

Possible Conclusions

A Rugby is another game that resembles football.

B Any way you kick and call it, some kind of football is popular almost everywhere.

C Football is fun!

D In conclusion, football can be found in many countries.

 Write a strong conclusion for the following paragraph.

How people dress depends on where they live. For example, in some Polynesian cultures, long grasses can be made into cool garments for the steamy weather. Alpaca wool, which is warm but lightweight, keeps Andeans both insulated and mobile in their cool mountain environment. Animal fur protects Siberians from their harsh winters.

Advice

You may be asked to give **advice**, or specific suggestions for solving a problem. Advice columnists give advice every day as they respond to people's letters. They use logic and what they know about a situation to draw conclusions and suggest a plan of action. Use similar strategies when you give advice.

It is logical to conclude that Plant Club will interest someone who likes plants.

Details give a new student information about Plant Club.

Suggestions give specific actions to help make friends.

Advice from Alison

Dear Terry,

Welcome to Wilshire Elementary School! You say in your letter that you are interested in plants and computers. Wilshire has an active Plant Club that meets after school on Tuesdays in the greenhouse. Kids in this club learn about growing and caring for plants. Twice a year, they take plants they have grown to nursing homes around town.

As a fifth grader, you'll have six weeks of computer class in the spring. You'll learn about software and the Internet. Ms. Punti tells some funny jokes too!

As for making friends, kids at Wilshire are friendly. Just be sure you wear a smile to school. Also, ask people for help in learning new routines. Once you start talking, you'll soon find friends who fit you like a glove!

Good luck!

Alison

Using *Who* and *Whom*

People sometimes confuse the pronouns *who* and *whom* when they write. *Who* is a subject form. It is used as a subject of a sentence or clause.

>*Who* made this mess?

>I saw a performer *who* could do four back flips. (*Who* is the subject in the dependent clause *who could do four back flips.*)

Whom is an object form. It is used as the object of a preposition or as a direct object.

>To *whom* did you send a letter?

>*Whom* will you ask?

In the first example, *whom* is the object of the preposition *to*. In the second example, *whom* is a direct object.

- The subject *(you)* often does not come first in a question. Don't be fooled if the subject does not come first.

- To understand why *Whom* is used in the second sentence, change the word order so that the subject comes first. (*Whom will you ask?* becomes *You will ask whom?*) This makes it easier to see that *whom* is a direct object.

Ⓐ How is the underlined word used? Write *subject, object of preposition,* or *direct object*.

>**1.** <u>Who</u> asked for athletic tape?

>**2.** That is the gymnast with <u>whom</u> I study.

>**3.** He is an athlete <u>who</u> once tried out for the Olympic team.

>**4.** <u>Whom</u> have you told?

>**5.** I told my cousin, <u>who</u> is only eleven.

B Choose the correct word in ( ). Write *who* or *whom* on your paper.

1. To (who, whom) do you wish to speak?

2. (Who, Whom) is that on the dance floor?

3. My brother, (who, whom) is a good dancer, says he will teach me.

4. The partner with (who, whom) he dances most often is Fiona.

5. A person (who, whom) has a good sense of rhythm usually can dance well.

6. (Who, Whom) will you ask to the dance?

7. The redheaded twins, (who, whom) are Irish, are taking step dancing lessons.

8. The teacher from (who, whom) she took ballet lessons had been a prima ballerina.

C Rewrite each pair of sentences as a complex sentence. Change one of the sentences into a dependent clause using *who* or *whom*.

Example Charlene is a determined young lady. She wants to be a championship skater.

Charlene is a determined young lady who wants to be a championship skater.

9. Janine is a strong swimmer. She specializes in the Australian crawl.

10. The Olympic competitors were participating in the diving events. I watched them.

11. Many divers compete on an international level. They have trained and practiced for countless hours.

12. The two swimmers stood motionless on the blocks. Everyone had been talking about them.

Test Preparation

✒ Write the letter of the answer that tells how the underlined word is used in the sentence.

1. <u>Who</u> is your favorite skater?

   A object of preposition
   B adjective
   C direct object
   D subject

2. To <u>whom</u> shall we give the food?

   A subject
   B object of preposition
   C direct object
   D noun

3. <u>Whom</u> shall we invite to the party?

   A direct object
   B verb
   C subject
   D object of preposition

Write the letter of the sentence that is correct.

4. **A** Whom has she chosen?
   B With who did he compete?
   C She is a coach whom helps everyone.
   D Whom started first?

5. **A** Leon told everyone whom qualified.
   B Beth, whom is my friend, moved.
   C Whom is his partner?
   D There is the boy who lost his skates.

6. **A** Mom asked, "Whom can help me?"
   B Everyone who was there helped her.
   C She asked the girl whom smiled.
   D Who would you ask?

Review

Write *subject, object of preposition,* or *direct object* to identify how the underlined word is used in the sentence.

1. <u>Who</u> is the dancer in the pink dress?
2. With <u>whom</u> did you study?
3. Margot is the dancer <u>who</u> won last year.
4. <u>Whom</u> will she choose as her partner?
5. People <u>who</u> are flexible can move more freely.
6. For <u>whom</u> have you called?
7. <u>Whom</u> did you interview from the dance company?
8. <u>Who</u> sprained his ankle?
9. The dancer about <u>whom</u> he wrote the article retired from the company last year.
10. The lead in the new production is a dancer <u>whom</u> the choreographer chose personally.

Write *who* or *whom* to complete each sentence correctly.

11. (Who, Whom) wants a career as a dancer?
12. Dancers are professionals (who, whom) must be in shape.
13. Anyone (who, whom) wants this career must work hard.
14. (Who, Whom) do you admire most of all modern dancers?
15. My sister, (who, whom) studied ballet, had to give up her career because of injury.
16. That dancer is someone about (who, whom) I have read.
17. Young dancers need an instructor with (who, whom) they are comfortable.
18. (Who, Whom) could we interview about this career?
19. We need someone (who, whom) will be honest.
20. (Who, Whom) would like to dance with me?

Sensory Details

Sensory details appeal to the reader's senses—sight, hearing, smell, taste, and touch. By using these details, writers help readers visualize what they are describing.

Sight	golden hair, snowy mountaintop
Hearing	shrill voice, screeching brakes
Smell	musty dungeon, smoky odor
Taste	tart apple, spicy soup
Touch	sticky jar, smooth silk

 Write the sense to which each sentence mainly appeals.

> sight   hearing   smell   taste   touch

1. The air was thick with the scent of cheap perfume.
2. My throbbing toe made it painful to walk.
3. The immaculate room was neat and tidy but expressed no personality.
4. The fresh orange juice was as sweet as nectar.
5. Gigantic steel skyscrapers rose from the streets like high cliffs.
6. A steady patter of rain lulled me to sleep.
7. The odor of hyacinths filled the room.
8. Sirens screeched through the city streets.
9. A few thin clouds drifted in the blue sky.
10. Who put all that salt in the soup?

 Write four sentences about eating pancakes, pizza, apples, or your favorite food. Appeal to at least four of the reader's senses.

Writing for Tests

Describe a time when you achieved a goal that was important to you. Use precise nouns, strong action verbs, and vivid adjectives to tell how you accomplished your goal. Use language that appeals to the senses.

Adjectives and precise nouns create a clear picture. ——

Details appeal to the senses of touch and sight. ——

Strong, exact verbs make the actions clear.

How I Learned to Ride Bareback

I was determined to ride a horse bareback, like the cowboys I'd seen in drawings. First, I had to find a way to mount our sleepy brown mare, Ladybug. As I stood next to her, Ladybug's gigantic frame loomed over me like a mountain.

Her velvet muzzle snuffled my hand and her brown eyes invited me to come aboard. But how could I get on her? My first move was to leap up, grab her mane, and throw my right leg over her back.

My next thought was to let Ladybug do the work. I struggled to pull myself up by her mane, but Ladybug shook her head and slipped her mane free. I'm not sure, but I think her snort was actually laughter!

Finally, I decided that Ladybug and I needed to work as a team. I saw a tree stump in the back of the yard and got a great idea. Using the stump as a launching pad, I boosted myself high enough to throw my leg over Ladybug's back. Then I pulled myself up by her mane. Success at last! Ladybug gave another snort and away we went!

Contractions and Negatives

A **contraction** is a shortened form of two words. An **apostrophe** is used to show where one or more letters have been left out. Some contractions are made by combining pronouns and verbs: *I + will = I'll; she + is = she's.* Other contractions are formed by joining a verb and *not: do + not = don't; are + not = aren't.*

- *Won't* and *can't* are formed in special ways *(can + not = can't; will + not = won't).*

Negatives are words that mean "no" or "not": *no, not, never, none, nothing.* Contractions with *n't* are negatives too. To make a negative statement, use only one negative word.

No   Don't never get in his way. There wasn't nobody here.
Yes Don't ever get in his way. There wasn't anybody here.

- Use positive words, not negatives, in a sentence with *not:*

Negative	Positive	Negative	Positive
nobody	anybody, somebody	nothing	anything, something
no one	anyone, someone	nowhere	anywhere, somewhere
none	any, all, some	never	ever, always

A Write the contraction for each pair of words.

1. you have	**7.** will not	**13.** I will
2. could have	**8.** we are	**14.** who will
3. he would	**9.** has not	**15.** I am
4. who has	**10.** did not	**16.** cannot
5. she has	**11.** they are	**17.** he is
6. it is	**12.** should not	**18.** you are

B Choose the correct word in ( ) to complete each sentence.

1. A hundred years ago, there weren't (any, no) superhighways.
2. The automobile was a new invention that most people didn't think would (never, ever) amount to much.
3. You couldn't travel (anywhere, nowhere) in a car without scaring horses pulling wagons and buggies.
4. (Anyone, No one) who had car trouble could not rely on a mechanic for repairs.
5. There weren't (any, no) car repair garages.
6. (No one, Someone) who bought a car for transportation was not considered sane.
7. You couldn't (never, ever) rely on your car to get you where you needed to go.
8. As you sped along at 20 miles per hour, a bystander would call out, "Don't you know (no, any) better? Get a horse!"

C Write the paragraph. Change the underlined phrases to contractions. Correct any errors with negatives.

(**9**) One day I will be a pilot. (**10**) I do not think nothing could be more thrilling than flying above the clouds. (**11**) When I am an adult, there probably will not be no nearby planets uninhabited by humans. (**12**) No one would never think twice about flying to Mars, so I would take my whole family there for a vacation. (**13**) However, I would not mind staying close to Earth, either. (**14**) There is not nothing quite as breathtaking as Earth seen from a plane. (**15**) There is the vast blue ocean twinkling with sunlight below me. (**16**) I cannot imagine nowhere more beautiful.

Test Preparation

Write the letter of the contraction that correctly completes each sentence.

1. ____ you ever wanted to go on a safari?

   A Have'nt   C Havent
   B Haven't   D Haveno't

2. ____ especially enjoy the jungle animals.

   A I'ld   C Id'
   B Id   D I'd

3. ____ we find any lions?

   A Can't   C Cant
   B Cann't   D Wont

4. ____ lucky if you see elephants.

   A Your   C You're
   B Youre   D You'are

Write the letter of the contraction that correctly completes each sentence.

5. ____ have a camera?

   A Doesn't anyone
   B Don't no one
   C Doesn't nobody
   D Hasn't no one

6. You ____ without one.

   A shouldn't go anywhere
   B shouldn't go nowhere
   C should not go nowhere
   D can't go nowhere

7. ____ of your pictures turn out?

   A Didn't none
   B Hadn't none
   C Don't none
   D Didn't any

8. I ____ to damage my pictures.

   A don't want nothing
   B don't want anything
   C do not want nothing
   D didn't want nothing

Review

Finish the equation. Write the contraction formed by the two words on the left.

1. who + will =
2. should + have =
3. we + are =
4. will + not =
5. can + not =
6. he + would =
7. they + are =
8. could + not =
9. did + not =
10. she + will =

Write the word in ( ) that correctly completes each sentence.

11. Haven't you (ever, never) dreamed of having a grand adventure?
12. There is not (any, no) shortage of adventurers in America's past.
13. There were many men and women who couldn't stand the idea of (anyone, no one) beating them.
14. Weren't (any, none) of these adventurers women?
15. Elizabeth Blackwell didn't have (no, any) role models when she studied medicine.
16. Despite hardship and prejudice, she didn't let (anyone, no one) keep her from becoming the first woman doctor in the United States.
17. Amelia Earhart was an aviation pioneer who was not afraid of (any, no) risk.
18. She died trying to fly around the world, and her plane wasn't (ever, never) found.
19. Hasn't (no one, anyone) ever tried to solve the mystery?
20. Yes, many people looked, but no one ever found (nothing, anything).

Support Your Argument

Support your **argument**—an opinion or position on an issue—with convincing reasons and evidence.

Read the opinion. Then write the numbers of the reasons that support the argument with convincing evidence.

Argument: Our family should get a dog as a pet.

1. Studies show that pets are good for relieving stress. According to research, dogs in particular help people relax and enjoy life.

2. Dogs need space, time, and a lifelong commitment. A dog depends completely on its owners for food, water, shelter, exercise, health care, and attention.

3. My friend Billy was bit by her cousin's dog, but that was just because she picked on it. If you treat a dog with firm kindness, it will be obedient.

4. Dogs are loyal and obedient and have even been known to save their owners' lives. I read an article about a German Shepherd that barked until its owner woke up to find the house on fire. Everyone got out alive.

5. The strong bond between a dog and its family enriches the lives of both. Dog owners will tell you that their dog is a beloved member of the family.

In a paragraph, tell which is a better pet: a dog or a cat. Support your opinion with reasons and evidence.

Editorial

In an **editorial**, a writer tries to persuade readers to agree with him or her. An editorial states the writer's opinion about an issue and offers evidence such as facts and examples to support the argument.

Writer states opinion right away.

Opposing argument is mentioned and then disproved by facts and examples.

Evidence from reliable sources supports writer's argument.

TV Forever!

To those people who say that TV is "on the way out" and will be replaced by Web sites, I say, "You are wrong!"

It is true that the traditional "big three" broadcasters are losing viewers. However, no one has to settle for the tired programs on ABC, NBC, and CBS anymore. There are hundreds of cable channels that cater to every interest. Music lovers can watch MTV. Animal lovers can view nature shows. History lovers can tune in one of the history channels. Budding chefs can watch any kind of chef prepare any kind of food.

Web sites are drawing millions, but they are not drawing people away from TV. Statistics show that TV is still a primary source of entertainment in America. The Nebraska Chronicle reports that 68 percent of the Omaha teenagers polled watch TV more than twenty-two hours a week—and the viewing hours are rising annually. Media specialist Rubin Shiff says, "TV is molding public thought and taste more than ever. It has a headlock on the American mind."

Adjectives and Articles

An **adjective** describes a noun or pronoun. It tells what kind, how many, or which one.

What Kind	huge, luxurious ship
How Many	2,200 passengers; many minutes
Which One	that iceberg

The **articles** *a, an,* and *the* appear before nouns or other adjectives.

- Use **a** before words that begin with a consonant sound: a lifeboat, a tragic shipwreck.

- Use **an** before words that begin with a vowel sound or a silent *h*: an hour, an awful sound.

- Use **the** before words beginning with any letter: the anchor, the satin shoes.

An adjective formed from a proper noun is a **proper adjective**. Proper adjectives are capitalized: British ship.

A Write *what kind, how many,* or *which one(s)* to tell which question each underlined adjective answers about a noun.

1. The giant ship had collided with an iceberg.

2. About 700 passengers survived.

3. Some people believed the ship was unsinkable.

Write *a, an,* or *the* to complete each sentence. Use the article that makes sense.

4. ____ *Titanic*'s hull was divided into 16 compartments.

5. As ____ result of the collision, six compartments flooded.

6. For ____ "unsinkable" ship, the *Titanic* sank rather quickly.

B Write each sentence. Underline the adjectives and circle the articles.

   1. A dive to the ocean floor takes you to another world.

   2. You move with a dreamlike slowness among the slippery inhabitants of the deep.

   3. Many strange animals and plants drift around you.

   4. Fish of every size and shape wind through long ribbons of graceful seaweed.

   5. Large and small dramas are acted out on this watery stage.

   6. Perhaps you will see a fearsome shark with razor-sharp teeth.

   7. You could hear the complex, eerie whistles and moans of whales.

   8. Thousands of different kinds of life flourish beneath the ocean.

C Add your own adjectives and articles to complete each sentence. Write the sentences.

   9. About ____ years ago, ____ galleon sailed from Mexico.

   10. ____ crew labored busily on ____ decks and in ____ riggings.

   11. In ____ cargo was ____ treasure of ____ gold and silver.

   12. Suddenly, ____ ship flying ____ skull and crossbones appeared.

   13. ____ battle took place, with ____ cannons roaring and ____ swords flashing.

   14. ____ galleon was hit by ____ cannonballs and sank into ____ depths.

   15. ____ treasure is still resting in ____ compartments of ____ galleon, waiting for ____ divers to discover it.

Test Preparation

✓ Write the letter that identifies an adjective in each sentence.

1. Spanish conquistadors sailed to the New World.

    A Spanish
    B conquistadors
    C sailed
    D New World

2. They were searching for fabulous wealth.

    A They   **C** for
    B were   **D** fabulous

3. The long voyage was dangerous and frightening.

    A and   **C** voyage
    B long   **D** was

4. Legends had told of seven cities filled with treasure.

    A Legends   **C** seven
    B told   **D** treasure

5. The Aztecs had a prosperous kingdom.

    A prosperous   **C** had
    B kingdom   **D** Aztecs

6. They had built a complex city on a shallow lake.

    A had   **C** city
    B built   **D** shallow

7. The ruler possessed vast stores of gold and silver.

    A ruler   **C** stores
    B vast   **D** silver

8. The conquerors changed a whole way of life.

    A conquerors   **C** whole
    B changed   **D** way

Review

 Write *what kind, how many,* or *which one(s)* to tell what question each underlined adjective answers about a noun.

1. Climbing a mountain is a <u>great</u> adventure.
2. <u>These</u> climbers have supplies for a month.
3. They have hired <u>several</u> Sherpas for assistance on the climb.
4. The Tibetan Sherpas are often <u>better</u> climbers than the people they assist.
5. They know which approaches are <u>safest</u>.
6. Near the top of a peak, a <u>few</u> small errors can be fatal.
7. Climbing upward requires <u>tremendous</u> effort.
8. <u>Numerous</u> climbers have fallen to their deaths or frozen in storms.
9. Nonetheless, they cannot resist the challenge of a <u>huge</u> mountain.
10. Danger is part of the thrill of the <u>snowy</u> slopes.
11. More and more people are seeking <u>that</u> thrill.
12. Perhaps <u>those</u> seekers should try looking closer to home.

 Write *a, an,* or *the* to complete each sentence. Choose the article that makes sense and follows the rules for articles.

13. Could you scale ____ icy cliffs in this area?
14. I would need ____ pick and some good climbing ropes.
15. ____ truth is, I'd be afraid to climb a mountain.
16. Sir Edmund Hillary was ____ honored climber.
17. He was one of ____ first men to scale Mount Everest.
18. This was and is ____ incredible feat.
19. I am ____ admirer of Sir Edmund.
20. He was ____ courageous man.

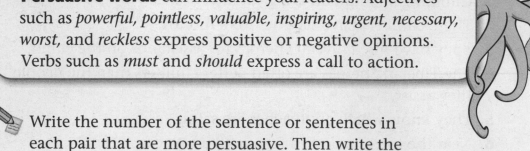

WRITER'S CRAFT

Use Persuasive Words

> **Persuasive words** can influence your readers. Adjectives such as *powerful, pointless, valuable, inspiring, urgent, necessary, worst,* and *reckless* express positive or negative opinions. Verbs such as *must* and *should* express a call to action.

Write the number of the sentence or sentences in each pair that are more persuasive. Then write the persuasive words in those sentences.

1. I want this bike because it is bright red and will last a long time.

2. The GX180 has a strong frame, sturdy tires, and powerful brakes. It is a superior bike.

3. The stop sign at Fourth and Oak Streets is not doing the job. A stoplight could be placed there instead.

4. Our community urgently needs to replace the stop sign at Fourth and Oak Streets with a stoplight. Cars stopped there cannot see oncoming traffic. We must create a safer situation before a tragic accident occurs.

 Use the words below or your own words to complete each sentence. Write a final sentence using a persuasive word.

healthier	safer	important	polluted	noisy	precious

Opinion: We should walk and use public transportation when possible.

This would cause less traffic and improve the (**5**) _____ air. Our (**6**) _____ downtown area would be peaceful. We could conserve (**7**) _____ resources. Best of all, there would be (**8**) _____ people and a (**9**) _____ environment. Walk or take a bus and see (**10**) _____ effects. _____

Problem-Solution Essay

> A **problem-solution essay** tells about a problem and suggests a way to solve it. Describe the problem first. Think about all the aspects of the solution to be sure it will really solve the problem.

Problem is clearly stated in introduction.

Specific, positive words persuade readers plan is sound.

Questions set off every aspect of plan, adding interest.

Walking Our Way to the Grand Canyon

Scout Troop 335 is planning a wilderness hike in the Grand Canyon. However, we have to raise $2,000 for this important trip. How can we raise the money?

It makes sense to have a nonstop 100-mile fundraising walk in Henry Forest Preserve. Henry Forest Preserve has clear, safe trails. The walk would help us get in excellent shape for our wilderness hike.

How could we walk so far without stopping? We would form a team and always have at least two scouts hiking. Others could rest until their turn. A turn could be one or two hours.

How would this event make money? We could ask sponsors to pledge money. We have 20 scouts. If every scout won the support of 10 sponsors, and every sponsor pledged $10, we would have our $2,000! We need your pledge for a successful fundraiser.

This, That, These, and *Those*

The adjectives *this, that, these,* and *those* tell which one or which ones. *This* and *that* modify singular nouns. *These* and *those* modify plural nouns. *This* and *these* refer to objects that are close by. *That* and *those* refer to objects farther away.

<u>This</u> classroom is brighter than <u>that</u> one across the hall.

<u>These</u> students at our table are my friends. <u>Those</u> students over there are new.

- Do not use *here* or *there after this, that, these,* or *those.*

No   <u>This here</u> book is about astronauts. <u>That there</u> one is about space.

Yes   <u>This</u> book is about astronauts. <u>That</u> one is about space.

- Do not use *them* in place of *those.*

No   She wrote <u>them</u> books for children.

Yes   She wrote <u>those</u> books for children.

A Write the word in ( ) that completes each sentence correctly.

1. (That, Those) movie tells about the flight of *Apollo 13.*
2. (This, These) story shows how three astronauts survived.
3. (That, This) picture I am holding is dramatic.
4. It was the 1960s, and in (these, those) days space travel was new.
5. Look at (these, this) pictures of a space capsule.
6. The first astronauts lived in (that, these) tiny space.
7. Will you proofread (this here, this) report on space travel?
8. For information, I looked in (them, those) new reference books at the learning center.

B Write *C* if the sentence is correct. If the words *this*, *that*, *these*, or *those* are used incorrectly, rewrite the sentence with the correct word.

1. Those sunset is colorful.

2. I think those farthest clouds are the kind called nimbus.

3. I'll use these camera to take a picture of the sunset.

4. Do you remember that day last year when we flew across the country from east to west?

5. This here sunset reminds me of the one we saw from the plane.

6. Them pictures of space were taken by the Hubble telescope.

7. These photograph of the moons of Saturn is especially interesting.

8. That there stack of magazines on the shelf shows more pictures of space.

9. Have you ever thought about traveling into those territory?

10. Them brave men and women who fly in space must see our world with different eyes.

11. That astronauts may not get a chance to go into space.

12. They were willing to wait for that opportunity.

C Space travel brings exciting new technology to the world. Use the following phrases to build sentences describing new technology you imagine in the future. Use *this*, *that*, *these*, and *those* correctly.

13. this new telescope

14. these lighter-than-air shoes

15. those bubble domes on Mars

16. that personal space vehicle

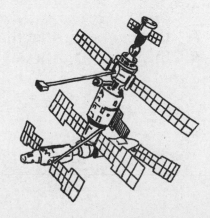

Test Preparation

Write the letter of the adjective that best completes each sentence.

1. ___ book is so heavy I can hardly lift it.

  A This   **C** Those
  B This here   **D** These

2. ___ mountains don't look that far away.

  A This   **C** These
  B That   **D** Those

3. I like ___ pictures better than those.

  A this   **C** these
  B that   **D** those

4. ___ car at the far end of the lot is mine.

  A This   **C** These
  B That   **D** Those

5. Please take ___ note to the office.

  A this   **C** that there
  B them   **D** these

6. I like the feel of ___ fabric.

  A this here   **C** those
  B this   **D** that there

7. In ___ early days, space travel was a dream.

  A this   **C** them
  B that   **D** those

8. Some believed ___ dream could be a reality.

  A these   **C** that
  B that there   **D** those

9. ___ days, we believe humans will go to Mars.

  A This   **C** These
  B That   **D** Those

10. ___ change is due to our astronauts.

  A This   **C** These here
  B That there   **D** Them

Review

 Write the word in ( ) that completes each sentence correctly.

1. (This, These) aircraft is called a helicopter.
2. Do you see (them, those) rotor blades on the top?
3. When they spin, (these, these here) blades provide lift.
4. (Those, those there) rotor blades on the tail prevent the helicopter from spinning out of control.
5. All aircraft obey (this, that) law: For every action there is an equal and opposite reaction.
6. The main rotors want to spin the aircraft one way, but (them, those) rear rotors create a force in the opposite direction.
7. I think this helicopter is more difficult to fly than (that, that there) plane.
8. To fly (this, these) machines, a helicopter pilot must manage three sets of controls at once.
9. (This, These) fact makes flying a helicopter a challenge for the most skilled pilot.
10. You can ride in (that, those) helicopter at the county fair for twenty-five dollars.

 Correct any mistakes in the use of *this, that, these,* and *those.* Write each sentence correctly.

11. Them helicopters are used by broadcasters to monitor traffic.
12. Did you know that these here aircraft did not become common until the 1940s?
13. In 1907, a pilot flew a helicopter for the first time, but those flight of his lasted only a few seconds.
14. That there craft crashed, but then advances came quickly.
15. Today this odd-looking crafts often can be seen in the sky.

Use Quotations

> **Quotations** are a person's exact words in print. Good writers use quotations to add interest and develop character.

Choose the quotation from the box that best fits each paragraph. Write the quotation correctly.

> She says, "Lots of people have to be away from their families because of their jobs."
>
> "Thanks to e-mail," Ochoa says, "when I am in space, my husband and I are able to communicate every day."
>
> She advises, "Get involved in activities where you work closely with other people."

1. Ellen Ochoa is a mother as well as an astronaut. She thinks that both of these full-time jobs call for hard work if they are to be done well. While she misses her family when in space, Ochoa reminds us that she is one of many parents who travel for work.

2. What advice does Ochoa have for aspiring young astronauts? She advises them to get a college degree in math. She points out, though, that there is more than math and science to being an astronaut. The job calls for teamwork and leadership.

3. How does Ochoa keep in touch with her family when she is in space? She cannot phone them, and there is no mail delivery. However, the space shuttle is in constant communication with Earth by computer.

Write about something a friend enjoys doing. Include a quotation from your friend about this activity.

Biographical Sketch

A **biographical sketch** focuses on a high point or an achievement in a person's life. It includes key facts and descriptions that characterize the person.

Reaching for the Stars

Descriptive details characterize Ochoa.

Through hard work, Ellen Ochoa became the first Hispanic American woman to go into space. Ochoa's role model was her mother, who worked hard for years to get her own college degree. When Ochoa attended college, her interests evolved from music and business to physics.

Facts help readers follow Ochoa's career.

Ochoa always loved the idea of going into space. However, she never thought of becoming an astronaut until 1978, when NASA chose six women for the space program. Ochoa began her formal training for space in 1990. After three years of preparing for any emergency that might occur, she went on her first mission.

Quotation by Ochoa summarizes her inspirational life and attitude.

Ochoa loves the excitement of traveling into space, although she misses her family. Back on Earth, she has become a role model for kids. She says, "It's important they know that if they work hard, they can be and accomplish whatever they want."

Comparative and Superlative Adjectives

Comparative adjectives are used to compare two people, places, things, or groups. Add *-er* to most short adjectives to make their comparative forms. Use *more* with longer adjectives. **Superlative adjectives** are used to compare three or more people, places, things, or groups. Add *-est* to most short adjectives to make their superlative forms. Use *most* with longer adjectives.

Adjective	Comparative	Superlative
strange	strang<u>er</u>	strang<u>est</u>
terrible	<u>more</u> terrible	<u>most</u> terrible

- Adjectives such as *good* and *bad* have irregular comparative and superlative forms: *good, better, best; bad, worse, worst.*
- Never use *more* or *most* with *-er* and *-est.*

  No   more angrier, most remarkablest
  Yes   angrier, most remarkable

A Write the comparative and superlative forms for each adjective.

1. deep
2. fat
3. bad
4. hideous
5. immense
6. mighty
7. wild
8. unbelievable
9. warm
10. tiny

11. colorful
12. good
13. scary
14. big
15. small
16. sharp
17. thrilling
18. early
19. fine
20. beautiful

B Write the forms of the adjectives in ( ) that correctly complete the sentences.

1. This is the ___ (good) book I have ever read.

2. It is even ___ (exciting) than watching a movie.

3. I usually find novels ___ (easy) to read than nonfiction.

4. As a hero's troubles get ___ (bad) than before, the ___ (interested) I become.

5. To me, science fiction is the ___ (thought-provoking) kind of writing of all.

6. Science fiction writers look even ___ (deep) into the future than scientists.

7. Science fiction is ___ (imaginative) and less concerned with scientific method than science.

8. In science fiction, even the ___ (wild) inventions of all still have some basis in scientific thought.

C Use the comparative or superlative form of an adjective from the box to complete each sentence. Write the sentence.

believable	close	admirable	loud

9. In these ten books you've read, which fictional character is ___, or worthy of respect?

10. Most readers feel ___ to a hero with problems than to one who is perfect.

11. Character flaws can often make a hero ___ to us than an unrealistic, flawless champion would be.

12. Readers save their ___ cheers of all for heroes who overcome problems.

Test Preparation

✓ Write the letter of the adjective form that best completes each sentence.

1. Which of these two stories do you like ____?

   A more better

   B better

   C best

   D most best

2. Adam's story is ____ than mine.

   A scary

   B more scary

   C scarier

   D scariest

3. My characters are ____ than his.

   A interestinger

   B more interesting

   C interestingest

   D most interesting

4. Which movie has the ____ monsters of all?

   A more realistic

   B realistic

   C most realistic

   D realistickest

5. Some monsters in old movies are ____ than scary.

   A amusing

   B more amusing

   C most amusing

   D amusingest

6. Isn't that Godzilla movie the ____ thing you ever saw?

   A worser

   B worsest

   C worse

   D worst

7. That monster looks ____ than a scared rabbit.

   A more tense

   B tenser

   C most tense

   D tensest

8. A monster in your imagination is ____ than one on the screen.

   A frightening

   B frighteningest

   C most frightening

   D more frightening

Review

If the adjective forms are correct, write *correct*. If they are not correct, write the comparative and superlative forms correctly.

Adjective	Comparative	Superlative
1. lovely	lovelyer	lovelyest
2. sad	more sadder	most saddest
3. incredible	incredibler	incrediblest
4. rough	more rough	most rough
5. bad	badder	baddest
6. lucky	luckier	luckiest

Write the correct forms of the adjectives in ( ) to complete the sentences.

7. Some of the _____ (grand) adventure stories in the world are fairy tales.

8. A young person sets off in search of a _____ (good) life than he or she had before.

9. This young hero always must face the _____ (great) trials possible.

10. Our hero is sure to meet the _____ (handsome) prince or _____ (beautiful) princess in the kingdom.

11. To win true love, the hero must achieve many goals, each one _____ (difficult) than the last.

12. The monster to be slain has already eaten most of the _____ (brave) and _____ (strong) young people in the land.

13. Often, a bit of magic will give the hero a _____ (great) advantage than others had.

14. The hero and his or her love go on to live the _____ (happy) life imaginable.

Know Your Audience

Before you write, always ask yourself, *Who are my readers? How much do they know about this subject? What are their interests? What kind of language is appropriate for them?* Then choose a subject, words, and details suitable for your audience.

 Read each paragraph. Think about word choice and details. Write the audience from the box that best matches each paragraph.

> parents   11-year-old pen pal

1. There are several reasons why we should become members of the Sci-Fi Thriller of the Month Club. First, I will read more books—something you are always telling me to do. Second, I will quit bugging you about being bored on weekends. Finally, these books will make me a better reader and thinker.

2. I was totally amazed to read that Jules Verne is your favorite author too. *20,000 Leagues Under the Sea* is also my favorite science fiction book. It is cool that we have so much in common.

 Imagine that your class is going to produce a play. You want your classmates to use a dramatic version of a particular story. Write a paragraph to persuade them that this story is the best choice.

Persuasive Letter

A **persuasive letter** uses reasons, facts, and examples to make a point. It also uses opinions and persuasive words such as *most important* to get the reader to do something.

Writer uses persuasive words (*should, everybody needs*).

Informal expressions appeal to a young reader.

Topic sentences focus on reasons.

Reasons are in order, with the final reason indicated as *most important*.

Escape to the Future

Dear Mike,

It's great that you'll have time to read a lot this summer. I think you should check out science fiction—the most awesome kind of books ever.

Everybody needs a little escape and excitement. Imagine journeying to Mars or surviving an attack by a giant squid on the ocean bottom. You are always on the go, so I know these action-packed, exciting stories will really grab you!

Science fiction also makes you wonder about the future. It shows where new technology might take us. What if computers were to replace teachers and schools?

Most important, many science fiction stories warn us about our mistakes. In one story, every living thing on Earth dies because of pollution. It made me think. We have to take care of our planet.

Run, don't walk, to get yourself some science fiction thrillers!

Your friend,

Ellen

Adverbs

Adverbs tell more about verbs. They explain *how, when,* or *where* actions happen. Many adverbs that tell *how* end in *-ly*. Adverbs can appear before or after the verbs they describe.

How	The time passed <u>slowly</u>. The dog waited <u>patiently</u>.
When	Travelers <u>seldom</u> stopped. <u>Yesterday</u> the stage came.
Where	Settlers moved <u>westward</u>. They built a town <u>here</u>.

Some adverbs tell more about an adjective or another adverb: Mining towns sprang up <u>very</u> quickly. They were <u>terribly</u> noisy.

Comparative adverbs compare two actions. Add *-er* to form a comparative adverb. **Superlative adverbs** compare three or more actions. Add *-est* to form a superlative adverb. If an adverb ends in *-ly*, use *more* or *most* instead of *-er* or *-est*.

Comparative Adverb	Miners worked <u>harder</u> than storekeepers.
Superlative Adverb	Farmers worked <u>hardest</u> of all. They depended <u>most completely</u> on the land and weather.

- The adverbs *well* and *badly* have special comparative and superlative forms: *well, better, best; badly, worse, worst.*

A Write the sentence. Underline the adverb. Circle the word it tells about.

1. The windmill turned lazily in the wind
2. Our footsteps echoed eerily in the empty building.
3. The third movie lasted longest of all.
4. Soon someone called the police.
5. The street was very still.

B Write the correct adverb in ( ) to complete each sentence.

1. When gold was discovered in California the stream of settlers flowed in (more quickly, most quickly) than before.

2. The California Gold Rush of 1849 increased the population (greatly, more greatly).

3. Many thousands of "'49ers" raced (eager, eagerly) to California.

4. A few miners became (incredible, incredibly) wealthy.

5. However, merchants made money (more consistently, most consistently) than miners did.

6. They succeeded (better, more better) than most gold seekers.

7. The gold seekers who did (worse, worst) of all often became drifters.

8. Many of them (not, never) went back east.

9. (Very, Often) they continued to search for gold.

C Add adverbs to make the sentences more lively and colorful. Write the sentences.

10. Early pioneers struggled ＿＿ and took ＿＿ great risks.

11. Most worked ＿＿ than they ＿＿ thought they could.

12. On the plains, settlers ＿＿ cut sod and ＿＿ built earthen homes.

13. A sod house would ＿＿ leak in a rainstorm, and the residents lived ＿＿ in their damp, muddy home.

14. When they were ＿＿ able, most settlers ＿＿ built wooden houses.

15. ＿＿, nature threw them difficult challenges, but the pioneers met these challenges ＿＿.

Test Preparation

✓ Write the letter of the word that is an adverb in each sentence.

1. The town desperately needs a tough, honest sheriff.

   A desperately   C tough
   B needs   D sheriff

2. A mysterious stranger rides silently into town.

   A mysterious   C rides
   B stranger   D silently

3. Soon he has pinned the sheriff's badge on his vest.

   A Soon   C pinned
   B has   D badge

4. He triumphs over the horribly cruel desperados.

   A triumphs   C horribly
   B desperados   D cruel

✓ Write the letter of the correct form to complete each sentence.

5. A villain appears even ____ than our hero did.

   A more mysteriously
   B mysteriouslier
   C most mysteriously
   D mysteriousliest

6. This bandit can draw ____ of all.

   A more quickly
   B most quickly
   C more quicklier
   D most quickliest

7. He and the hero ____ will settle their grudge.

   A final
   B more finally
   C most finally
   D finally

8. After settling the manner ____, our hero will ride out of town.

   A honorably
   B honorable
   C more honorably
   D most honorably

Review

 Fill in the chart. Write the comparative and superlative forms of each adverb.

Adverb	Comparative	Superlative
1. sadly		
2. hard		
3. slyly		
4. badly		
5. cheerfully		
6. fast		
7. quickly		
8. well		
9. long		
10. noisily		

 Write each sentence. Underline the adverb and circle the word or phrase it tells more about. One sentence contains two adverbs.

11. Trappers first traveled to the American West.

12. They eagerly sought the furs of beavers and muskrats.

13. These furs brought extravagantly high prices.

14. Trappers knew the Native Americans well.

15. They sometimes adopted the native way of life.

16. Theirs was a very solitary existence.

17. They knew the plants and animals of the West thoroughly.

18. Beavers became almost extinct because millions were trapped.

19. Later, hunters and military scouts recklessly slaughtered most of the buffalo.

20. The Plains Indian way of life vanished rapidly after that.

Style

The way you express yourself in writing is your own personal **style**. Choose interesting, exact words that are natural to you. Combine short, choppy sentences to develop your style.

Choppy   The transcontinental railroad was completed in 1869. It connected East and West. It sped up the settling of the West.

Improved   Completed in 1869, the transcontinental railroad sped up the settling of the West by connecting it with the East.

 Improve the style of these sentences by combining them into one interesting sentence.

1. The old cabin looked abandoned. It was broken down. Many windows were missing.

2. It had once been a mining cabin. Scattered picks, shovels, and pans showed this. Prospectors used it.

3. They left their equipment behind. This made me wonder. I wondered if they had given up in despair.

4. Today the cabin was inhabited. Something furry lived there. It had dug a den in the dirt floor.

 Write several sentences about a deserted town. Use precise words and a variety of sentences to create an interesting style.

Ad

An **ad** tries to persuade a reader to buy a product or service or to take a certain action. An ad relies on persuasive and descriptive words to appeal to the reader. It also provides logical and emotional reasons why the reader should buy or act.

Writer uses descriptive words that appeal to reader's senses.

Details inform and also suggest educational value of town.

A lively style brings activity to life for readers.

Wonderful Wilderton

Wilderton is a small, historic gem sparkling on the side of Mount Stanton. That delightful sound you hear is a clear mountain stream rushing past your hotel room.

Wander down Main Street and take a trip back in time. The General Store offers calico and old-fashioned ice cream sodas. Pause at Joe's Smithy Shop and watch an expert blacksmith at his forge. Hop on a genuine mining wagon and ride leisurely up the mountain to the Fargo Mine. This silver mine offers tours and tales about the heyday of silver mining.

Then relax and enjoy the evening in one of our twelve excellent restaurants. Hoot and holler to the rip-roaring song, dance, and comedy routines at Sam's Folly.

Wilderton is a fabulous reminder of the Wild West. You definitely won't want to leave!

Modifiers

Adjectives, adverbs, and prepositional phrases are **modifiers**, words or groups of words that tell more about, or modify, other words. Adjectives modify nouns and pronouns. Adverbs modify verbs, adjectives, or other adverbs. Prepositional phrases can act as adjectives or adverbs.

As Adjective The towel <u>with green stripes</u> is mine.

As Adverb A crab ran <u>under a rock</u>.

- To avoid confusion, place modifiers close to the words they modify. Adjective phrases usually come right after the word they modify. Adverb phrases may appear right after a verb or at the beginning of a sentence.

- Meaning can be unclear if a modifier is misplaced.

   No   The girl set out a picnic <u>in a red bathing suit</u>.

   Yes   The girl <u>in a red bathing suit</u> set out a picnic.

- The position of *only* in a sentence can also affect meaning. Place only directly before the word it modifies.

   Example   <u>Only</u> he ate oysters. (Nobody else ate them.)

   He <u>only</u> ate oysters. (He didn't do anything except eat.)

   He ate <u>only</u> oysters. (He ate nothing else.)

A Write adverb, adjective, or prepositional phrase to identify each underlined modifier.

1. We <u>always</u> visit the beach.
2. I love the <u>warm</u> sun.
3. A wave crashed <u>very</u> loudly.
4. I see a <u>tiny</u> jellyfish!
5. One stung me <u>on the foot</u>.

B Write each prepositional phrase. Tell whether it acts as an adverb or an adjective by writing *adv.* or *adj.* The number in ( ) tells how many prepositional phrases are in the sentence.

1. Near my house is a beautiful sand beach. (1)

2. Several members of my family jog on the wet sand. (2)

3. A sign with big red letters says, "Swim at your own risk." (2)

4. People of all ages fish and relax on the pier. (2)

5. Above the blue ocean water, parasailers soar toward the clouds. (2)

6. Sunbathers with towels and in lounge chairs nap in the sun or read books. (3)

7. Seagulls with broad wings flap and dive along the long sandy coastline. (2)

8. By late afternoon, most of the people have left. (2)

9. Sunsets of beautiful reds and oranges bring an end to many peaceful days. (2)

10. A runner is alone with the cries of the gulls. (2)

C Add adjectives, adverbs, and prepositional phrases to these sentences to create more specific, interesting statements. Reposition the misplaced modifiers that are in four sentences.

11. The children waited at a picnic table.

12. Their parents brought a picnic.

13. One boy drank lemonade.

14. We gave a girl some lotion with a sunburn.

15. Sara shrieked when a wave hit her loudly.

16. Two children chased a sandpiper with a net.

17. Of all the children, Mark had worn only sunscreen.

18. The parents packed the car.

Test Preparation

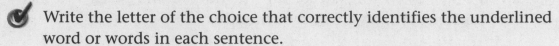

Write the letter of the choice that correctly identifies the underlined word or words in each sentence.

1. My cousin <u>especially</u> enjoys the beach.

  A adj.

  B adv.

  C adj. prep. phrase

  D adv. prep. phrase

2. We ride there <u>on our bikes</u>.

  A adj.

  B adv.

  C adj. prep. phrase

  D adv. prep. phrase

3. We stay <u>for the whole afternoon</u>.

  A adj.

  B adv.

  C adj. prep. phrase

  D adv. prep. phrase

4. We find treasures <u>of all types</u>.

  A adj.

  B adv.

  C adj. prep. phrase

  D adv. prep. phrase

5. We found a <u>weird</u> horseshoe crab shell.

  A adj.

  B adv.

  C adj. prep. phrase

  D adv. prep. phrase

6. It looked <u>very</u> strange.

  A adj.

  B adv.

  C adj. prep. phrase

  D adv. prep. phrase

Write the letter of the sentence that has a misplaced modifier.

7. **A** A boy with a stick poked a crab.

  B Did you get sand in your sandwich?

  C Thousands of jellyfish washed up on the beach.

  D We only could stay till 4 o'clock.

8. **A** That girl saw a dolphin in an inner tube.

  B It leapt from the water several times.

  C People shield their eyes from the sun.

  D The sunlight causes a glare on the water.

Review

 Write the three modifiers from each sentence. (Do not include articles.) Put adjectives and adjective phrases in one column and adverbs and adverb phrases in another column.

1. A gray bank of clouds loomed on the horizon.
2. A cold wind suddenly blew across the waves.
3. Forked spears of lightning danced from clouds.
4. Anxious parents called loudly to children.
5. Everyone on the beach ran under a canopy for shelter.
6. In minutes, only crabs were scurrying playfully.
7. A change in the weather can easily ruin a trip to the beach.
8. Cautious people always put an umbrella and a jacket in their bags.

 Write the sentences. Underline the adjectives and adverbs, and circle the prepositional phrases. Rewrite the two sentences with misplaced modifiers correctly. The number in ( ) tells how many modifiers are in each sentence.

9. These grains of sand came from sandstone. (3)
10. Over the centuries, wind and rain slowly wore the soft stone into gravel. (4)
11. The rich, dark soil of the plains was formed similarly. (4)
12. Organic matter and tiny pieces of rock gradually combine into soil. (5)
13. Roots hold the soil in place of plants. (2)
14. Sand is moved easily by wind and waves. (2)
15. You seldom see live plants on a beach. (3)
16. The couple watched a crab from New Mexico walk sideways. (2)

WRITER'S CRAFT

Thesis Statement

> A **thesis statement** expresses an essay's main idea.
> The essay develops and supports the idea.

 Read the paragraph below and the three sentences that follow it. Write the letter of the sentence that is the best thesis statement for the paragraph.

    The starfish has no front or back and can move in any direction without turning. Its five arms radiate out from the center. However, these appendages are not simply arms. They contain internal organs and canals that are part of the starfish's system for attaching itself to rocks. Stranger yet, a starfish is not doomed if it loses an arm or two. It can regrow missing body parts. Most startling of all, the starfish eats by turning its stomach inside out and pushing it into its prey's shell. It actually digests food outside its body!

  A Starfish are only one of the large groups of marine animals known as echinoderms.

  B Of all the marine creatures you are likely to find in a tide pool, the starfish is the most unusual.

  C Starfish are able to rearrange their arms in order to fit themselves into small openings in ocean rocks.

 Write a thesis statement for a paragraph about an interesting pet or other animal. Then write two or three pieces of information that you could include in your paragraph.

Expository Writing

> **Expository writing** explains and informs. Decide what your readers need to know about the subject. You may have to research information. State the important facts clearly. Organize the supporting details in a logical way.

Thesis statement summarizes focus of essay. ———

Specific words create clear picture of sea urchin's body. ———

Paragraphs discuss movement, feeding, and defending in order given in thesis statement.

Sea Urchin

The sea urchin is a marine animal with special ways of moving, feeding, and defending itself. These round animals have a hard shell with many sharp, movable spines. Between the spines, you can see tiny tube feet. The sea urchin uses suckers on these feet, along with its spines, to move itself slowly along the ocean floor.

Spines and tube feet also help the urchin hold food. Its mouth is on its bottom side. This is more convenient than it sounds. The urchin can use its teeth to scrape plant matter from rocks. It can even scrape a hole in a rock where it can hide from its predators!

If you step on a sea urchin, you will know it! The spines sting and are hard to remove. However, the sea urchin is only defending itself from its many predators. Even its cousin the starfish will eat a sea urchin.

Conjunctions

A **conjunction** is a word such as *and*, *or*, or *but* that joins words, phrases, or sentences.

- Use *and* to join related ideas: Deer <u>and</u> elk are similar animals.

- Use *but* to join contrasting ideas: The deer looks small <u>but</u> healthy.

- Use *or* to suggest a choice: Do deer eat more grass <u>or</u> leaves?

You can use conjunctions to make compound subjects, compound predicates, and compound sentences. Place a comma before the conjunction in a compound sentence.

Compound Subject	No wolves <u>or</u> bears lived there.
Compound Predicate	The deer herd thrived <u>and</u> grew.
Compound Sentence	The deer grew fat, <u>and</u> their numbers grew quickly.

A Write the conjunction in ( ) that correctly completes each sentence.

1. Deer eat green plants, (and, but) these are not available in winter.
2. Deer may have to eat bark (and, but) twigs instead.
3. Too much snow (but, or) ice can keep them from grazing.
4. Five deer tramped into the yard (and, or) ate from the bird feeder.
5. A strip mall went up nearby, (and, or) the deer lost their habitat.
6. Now the deer must look for food in yards, (but, or) they will go hungry.

B Write the conjunction in each sentence. Then write *compound subject, compound predicate*, or *compound sentence* to identify the parts that the conjunction joins.

1. Sheep and cattle are domesticated animals.

2. Domesticated animals depend on humans, and in return they provide humans with useful products.

3. Wild animals live on their own but depend on humans too.

4. People may not see these animals, but the animals have a profound impact on their lives.

5. Construction and pollution are two human causes of problems for animals.

6. However, people can also pass laws for endangered animals or create wildlife refuges.

C Combine the sentences using appropriate conjunctions. Write the new sentences. Add commas where needed.

7. Beavers are fun to watch. They can be destructive.

8. They cut down trees near a creek. They use these trees to build a dam.

9. Creek water floods the area. The habitat changes.

10. These changes are great for the beavers. They are frustrating for humans.

11. Would you want beavers living in your yard? Would you want them inhabiting a park used by lots of people?

12. The population of humans is growing. The population of wildlife is shrinking.

Test Preparation

✓ Write the letter of the choice that best completes each sentence.

1. I want to be either a zoologist _____ a photographer.

  A and   **C** or
  B but   **D** to

2. To photograph wildlife requires patience _____ skill.

  A and   **C** or
  B but   **D** because

3. Wild animals are wary _____ suspicious of humans.

  A until   **C** nor
  B but   **D** and

4. They must be alert, _____ they may become dinner!

  A so   **C** or
  B and   **D** but

5. In a zoo, animals gain safety _____ lose freedom.

  A and   **C** or
  B but   **D** because

6. I take pictures of birds _____ squirrels.

  A and   **C** while
  B but   **D** although

7. Should I use a zoom _____ a telephoto lens?

  A and   **C** or
  B but   **D** if

8. The bird saw me _____ quickly flew off.

  A and   **C** or
  B but   **D** so

9. That bird is a wren _____ a sparrow.

  A and   **C** but
  B however   **D** or

10. Bluebirds _____ cardinals are my favorites.

  A and   **C** or
  B but   **D** until

Review

Write the correct conjunction in ( ) to complete each sentence.

1. We saw some seals (and, or) seabirds sunning themselves on the rocks.

2. The seals moved awkwardly on land (and, but) gracefully in the water.

3. Are seals (but, or) dolphins easier to train?

4. I'd like to go to Sea World (and, but) will probably visit the Wild Animal Park instead.

5. The Wild Animal Park is quite large (and, or) allows animals to wander over a large area.

6. Would you rather watch the dolphins (but, or) the killer whales perform at Sea World?

Write the conjunction in each sentence and notice what sentence parts it joins. Write *compound subject, compound predicate*, or *compound sentence.*

7. Predators, disease, or starvation is a likely cause of death among wildlife.

8. Zoo animals are protected from these problems and are more likely to die of old age.

9. Wild animals enjoy freedom but usually live shorter lives.

10. Are they happier than zoo animals, or would they prefer a life of safe captivity?

11. Endangered species need protection, or they will soon become extinct.

12. More plants and animals become endangered over time.

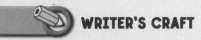

Paraphrase

When you take notes on facts in a book or article, you **paraphrase** the article. When you paraphrase, choose the most important facts and restate them in your own words.

- Paraphrase only the main ideas, not unimportant details. Make sure you paraphrase the facts correctly.
- Use your own words, not the words and word order used by the author.
- If a phrase or sentence is especially interesting, write it in quotation marks.

 Read the paragraph below. Write the letter of the item that is the best paraphrase of the paragraph.

When twenty-nine reindeer were released on Saint Matthew Island in 1944, the future of the herd seemed bright. This island in the midst of the Bering Sea offered plenty of plants and lichens for the reindeer to eat. No wolves, bears, or other large predators lived on the island. Biologists expected the herd to grow quickly, and it did. By 1963, just nineteen years later, the herd numbered more than six thousand animals.

A The herd of twenty-nine reindeer set free on Saint Matthew Island in 1944 grew and thrived because of favorable conditions there. By 1963 there were over six thousand reindeer.

B There were many plants on Saint Matthew Island in the Bering Sea but not many predatory animals. Reindeer were first brought to the island in 1944.

C The twenty-nine reindeer released on Saint Matthew Island in 1944 seemed to have a bright future. Biologists expected the herd to grow quickly, and by 1963 the herd numbered more than six thousand animals.

Taking Notes

Readers **take notes** to gather information they need to remember about a text. Note takers may summarize, or write down only the main ideas and most important supporting details. They may copy some words and put quotation marks around them to show the words are not their own. They may also paraphrase the ideas, or rewrite them in their own words. Here are one student's notes on the complete article referred to on page 210.

Writer used a chart to arrange notes.

Quotation marks show that these words are quoted directly from article.

Most sentences paraphrase and summarize information from article.

Notes on St. Matthew Island Mystery
How Dr. Klein found out when the reindeer died

Clues from Skeletons	What Clues Tell
All skeletons were in "the same state of decay."	All deer died at the same time.
Bones were bleached and mossy.	They likely died three years before.
Klein had visited in 1963. Then he saw 6,000 deer. Now it was 1966.	They must have died between 1963 and 1964.
Unborn baby reindeer were examined. Their bones were tiny and newly formed.	They had died while still inside their mothers. The female reindeer had died in late winter when their calves were still developing.

Conclusion All the deer died between February and March, 1964.

Commas

Commas can clarify meaning and tell readers when to pause.

- Put a comma after every item in a *series* but the last.

  King Midas turned roses, porridge, and a girl into gold.

  The king wept, moaned, and wrung his hands.

- When you speak or write to someone, you may use the person's name or title. This noun of *direct address* is set off with a comma, or two commas if it is in the middle of a sentence.

  What's wrong, Father?

  There's not a thing, dear, for you to worry about.

- *Appositives* are noun phrases that describe another noun. They are set off by commas.

  Ms. Wong, my favorite teacher, received an award.

- Put a comma after an *introductory word or phrase*, such as *yes, no, well, of course,* or *as usual.*

  Yes, I did enjoy the story. In fact, it is my new favorite.

A Rewrite each sentence. Add commas where they are needed.

1. Joan Mary and Wes want to turn the story into a play.
2. They will write dialogue plan sets and hold auditions.
3. Mr. Allen our music teacher will handle the sound effects.
4. Patty will you make the sets?
5. As usual Patty you have done a great job.
6. Who will play King Midas the most important role?
7. Jada's mom Mrs. Chandler will make costumes.
8. King Midas his daughter and the mysterious stranger need costumes.

B Each sentence contains comma errors. Rewrite the sentence, adding commas where they are needed and deleting commas where they are not needed.

1. Costumes props, and sets, all help create the atmosphere for a play.

2. Of course finding the right materials and using them effectively requires a lot of imagination.

3. Dylan will you make a cardboard crown, a paper, rose and some gold-colored coins?

4. Ms. Washington our costume designer will make a long cape and a dress.

5. Can we count on you Anita to help with the stage sets?

6. We will need to create, a dungeon an impressive throne room, and a garden.

7. Yes, Helen that armchair covered with gold fabric does look like a throne.

C Add the kind of words in ( ) to complete each sentence. Write the sentences using commas where they are needed.

8. (items in series) are three villains in fairy tales

9. (appositive) The main character in my favorite fairy tale faces many challenges.

10. Can you remember (direct address) who are the villains of these stories?

11. (direct address) will you act out this story with me?

12. (introductory word or phrase) we will have fun doing this!

13. Ms. Mason (appositive) said she would help us.

14. We need to (items in series) to get ready.

Test Preparation

✓ Write the letter of the choice that shows the words and punctuation needed to complete each sentence correctly.

1. _____ the curtain!

   A Pedro open

   B Pedro, open,

   C Pedro open,

   D Pedro, open

2. Speak _____ .

   A loudly, clearly, and distinctly

   B loudly clearly, and distinctly

   C loudly, clearly, and, distinctly

   D loudly clearly and distinctly

3. _____ tries to remember their lines.

   A Of course the cast

   B Of course, the cast

   C Of course, the cast,

   D Of course the cast,

4. _____ suffer from stage fright.

   A Gina, Jerry, and Brenda,

   B Gina Jerry, and Brenda

   C Gina, Jerry, and Brenda

   D Gina Jerry and Brenda

5. I will look for _____ in the audience.

   A you, Mom and Dad,

   B you Mom and Dad

   C you Mom, and Dad

   D you Mom, and Dad,

6. _____ seemed charged with electricity.

   A Indeed, the air,

   B Indeed the, air

   C Indeed the air,

   D Indeed, the air

Review

 Write the words in each sentence that should be followed by commas. Write the commas too.

1. People most often wish for money love and happiness.
2. Ryan what did King Midas wish for?
3. That's right he wanted every object that he touched to turn into gold.
4. Gold a precious metal is seen by many as an important form of wealth.
5. Most people believe that money will give them power freedom and respect.
6. What do you think Moira?
7. Can happiness that elusive quality be acquired with money?

 Each sentence contains comma errors. Write the sentence, adding commas where they are needed and removing unneeded commas.

8. Usually a magical being grants, wishes in a tale.
9. Animals genies, and fairies, can grant wishes.
10. A fisherman a poor man catches a magical fish.
11. The fish cries, "Please sir let me go, and I will grant you three wishes."
12. Yes the first two wishes are often foolish ones!
13. Of course these wishes bring bad consequences unhappiness and heartache.
14. The final wish a wise one is, often to return to life as it used to be.
15. Greed, ambition and selfishness, get in the way of happiness.

Figurative Language

Poems often contain **figurative language** such as similes, metaphors, and personification. Figurative language uses words to describe things in new and unusual ways. It is not meant to be taken literally.

- A *simile* compares two things you would not usually think of as being alike. It uses the word *like* or *as*.

- A *metaphor* compares two things without *like* or *as*.

- *Personification* gives human characteristics to an animal or an object.

Simile   His touch was like poison.

Metaphor   Her smile was a ray of sunlight.

Personification   The leaves were whispering to one another.

 Label each example of figurative language as a *simile*, *metaphor*, or *personification*.

    1. His heart was as heavy as a lump of gold.

    2. Her eyes were stars.

    3. The heavens wept.

    4. Stones danced in the waterfall.

 Add your own words to complete each figure of speech.

    5. Her laughter sounded like _____. (simile)

    6. Greed is like _____. (simile)

    7. Books are _____. (metaphor)

    8. The ocean _____. (personification)

Humorous Poem

The purpose of a **humorous poem** is to make readers smile or even laugh. Such poems may have any of the following:

- *rhyme* (words with the same ending sounds—*jolly holly*)
- *rhythm* (words with a regular beat—*Yankee Doodle went to town*)
- *alliteration* (words with the same beginning sounds—*popular pooch*)
- *hyperbole* (exaggeration for effect—*I could eat a hippopotamus.*)
- *similes* (comparisons with the words *like* and *as*—*hard as a rock*)
- *metaphors* (comparisons without *like* and *as*—*He is a rock.*)

Rhythm, rhyme scheme, and word choice create lighthearted mood.

Simile "sweet as a bride" creates vivid image.

Alliteration creates upbeat sound effects for ending.

Paula the Pooch and Her Magical Smooch

A jolly young poodle, my Paula, my pride,
can change you from sour to sweet as a bride
in less than a second. Believe me, it's true!
If you're sadder than sad or bluer than blue,

then Paula will dance her way up to your frown,
and with her pink tongue turn it upside down.
There isn't a Mr., a Ms., or a Mrs.
Who isn't made better by dozens of kisses.

I've heard of a goose and a king that made gold.
Rumpelstiltskin did too, or so I am told.
But there's no one who's richer than Paula the Pooch
with her magical, mystical, mirth-making smooch.

Quotations and Quotation Marks

A **direct quotation** gives a person's exact words and is enclosed in **quotation marks (" ")**. Direct quotations begin with capital letters and end with proper punctuation. End punctuation is inside the closing quotation marks. Words that tell who is speaking are set off from the quotation by punctuation.

- When the quotation comes last, set it off with a comma.

    Tony said, "I love reading about the history of flight."

- When the quotation comes first in a sentence, a comma, question mark, or exclamation mark sets off the quotation.

    "Have you read about dirigibles?" asked Norm.

- When the quotation is interrupted by words that tell who is speaking, use two sets of quotation marks. Words that tell who is speaking are followed by punctuation. Use a comma if the second part of the quotation does not begin a new sentence.

    "I understand," replied Tony, "that they were very large."

- Use end punctuation and a capital letter if the second part of the quotation does begin a new sentence.

A Write each sentence. Add quotation marks where needed.

  1. I'm flying to England this summer! exclaimed Robby.

  2. Ms. West asked, Have you ever flown across the Atlantic?

  3. No, I haven't, he said, but once I flew to Mexico.

  4. This flight will be longer, she said. It will take eight hours.

B Write each sentence correctly. Add quotation marks, capital letters, and punctuation where needed.

1. would you rather fly or take the train asked Melanie.

2. it depends replied Dana on how far I have to go

3. Brian commented my family took the train through the mountains last year

4. The views were just incredible he continued we had sleeper cars too

5. I like flying to distant places said Tamara it's much quicker and easier

6. When I fly she continued distances seem very small.

C Read each paragraph. Write the sentence from the box that supports each paragraph's ideas. Add quotation marks, capital letters, and punctuation where needed.

> a great engineer, Werner von Braun, declared it will free man from the chains of gravity which still tie him to this planet
>
> as pilot Antoine de Saint-Exupery said the airplane has unveiled for us the true face of the earth

7. Those who fly around the earth see it with a new perspective. It is not a group of countries separated by distinct boundaries. Instead, it is a seamless, unified sphere. Its blue oceans and green and brown areas of land support all kinds of life.

8. Once people could fly around the world, they turned their eyes to the moon. Surely it was possible to travel there? Some began to focus intensely on the next challenge: space flight.

Test Preparation

Write the letter of the choice that completes each sentence correctly.

1. "Who was the first man in ____ asked Zach.

    A space,"
    B space?"
    C space."
    D space,

2. "I think it was ____ answered Carmen.

    A John Glenn."
    B John Glenn"
    C John Glenn".
    D John Glenn,"

3. Ms. Bridgman ____ it was Yuri Gagarin."

    A said, "Actually,
    B said. "Actually,
    C said, "actually,
    D said, Actually

4. She continued, "John Glenn was the first American ____

    A in space".
    B in space,"
    C in space."
    D in space.

5. "Gagarin was a Russian ____ Ms. Bridgman told us.

    A astronaut."
    B astronaut,"
    C astronaut?"
    D astronaut"

6. Joey ____ didn't the United States get into space first?"

    A asked, "Why
    B asked? "Why
    C asked, "why
    D asked? "why

7. "We hadn't created the ____ she replied.

    A technology!
    B technology?"
    C technology,"
    D technology,

8. "Soon, though," she said, ____ dove into the space race."

    A "we
    B "We
    C we
    D We

Review

Write *C* if a sentence is correct. If it has errors in quotation marks, punctuation, or capital letters, rewrite the sentence correctly.

1. "Have you ever been surprised on a flight, asked Deanna?
2. "I was surprised by how neat the fields and buildings looked below," said Roger.
3. "They resembled a piece of artwork he went on.
4. "We once flew through a thunderstorm remarked Carlos."
5. "Please remain seated and keep your seatbelts fastened," the pilot announced. "We are encountering turbulence."
6. Rosa recalled. "I didn't know that we had to pay for our meals on the plane".
7. I also didn't realize that there would be so little leg room, she continued.
8. "All of the flight attendants, though," she remarked, "were very attentive."

Write each sentence correctly. Add quotation marks, capital letters, and punctuation where needed.

9. the clouds were a big surprise to me said Will as we passed through them, they seemed like smoke
10. looking down on the clouds gave me a very strange feeling he added
11. I didn't realize the change in air pressure would hurt my ears said Becky.
12. did you know asked Anthony that yawning helps you equalize the pressure

Include Important Details

When you outline information, first decide on the main ideas to include. You can use your main ideas to write topic sentences. To support your main ideas, be careful just to **include important details**. Irrelevant or unimportant details will weaken your writing.

Read each topic sentence. Write the letters of the details that support it.

1. In six years, the R101, a British dirigible, was planned, built, used, and destroyed.

   A Plans to construct the R101 were set in motion in 1924.

   B Also in 1924, the Goodyear Company started building two airships for the U.S. Navy.

   C Designed by Lt. Col. V. R. Richmond, the R101 was the largest rigid airship ever built.

   D It was put into service on October 14, 1929.

   E When the R101 crashed and burned in France on October 4, 1930, 48 of its 54 passengers died.

2. The word *dirigible*, a synonym for *airship*, comes from French.

   A The French verb *diriger* means "to control or steer."

   B The French adjective *dirigeable* is made from the verb *diriger*.

   C Airships are also sometimes called Zeppelins.

   D The French called a steerable lighter-than-air craft a *ballon dirigeable*.

   E English adapted the term and shortened it to *dirigible*.

Outlining

As you have seen, an **outline** is a way to summarize and organize information in a text. Main ideas are listed with Roman numerals (I, II, III, IV). Details that support each main idea are listed with the letters A, B, C, and so on. An outline helps you put your ideas in order before you write a research report. Here is one student's outline on an article about the *Hindenburg* airship.

The History of the *Hindenburg*

I. Dirigibles were huge airships that evolved into successful flying machines.

    A. The first dirigible flew in 1900.

    B. In 1931, the *Graf Zeppelin* began transatlantic flights.

    C. The biggest, most luxurious airship, *Hindenburg*, appeared in 1936.

    D. Designer Hugo Eckener worked hard to make it safe.

II. Against his will, Eckener had to bow to the Nazis who were rising to power.

    A. He criticized Nazi brutality and purpose.

    B. His ideal of service to mankind clashed with Nazi hunger for power and glory.

    C. He was made a "nonperson" and forced to fly the Nazi symbol on the *Hindenburg*.

Main ideas are indicated with Roman numerals.

Details under I explain, in chronological order, how dirigibles evolved.

Supporting statements relate to main idea statement in II.

Punctuation

You have already learned about commas, quotation marks, and end marks. Here are some other kinds of punctuation.

- A **colon (:)** is used to separate hours and minutes in expressions of time. It is also used after the salutation in a business letter.

     12:00 P.M.   9:35 A.M.   Dear Mr. Smith: Sir:

- A **hyphen (-)** is used in some compound words, such as numbers from twenty-one to ninety-nine and compound words that are thought of as one word.

     a ten-year-old rider   thirty-five   a high-class club

- A **semicolon (;)** can be used to join two independent clauses instead of a comma and a conjunction.

     Ben practiced piano faithfully; he became a fine pianist.

- **Italics** or **underlining** is used for titles of books, newspapers, magazines, and works of art. Because you cannot write italics, underline titles in your writing.

     Los Angeles Times or <u>Los Angeles Times</u> (newspaper)

- A **dash (—)** sets off information or a comment that interrupts the flow of a sentence.

     The shiny horn—the only new thing he had ever had—took his breath away.

A Rewrite each sentence. Add the missing punctuation marks.

  1. The note said, "Dear Ms. Imm Please arrive at 130 P.M."

  2. The New York Times is a top notch newspaper.

  3. The party it was for Grandma's sixty first birthday was to begin at 700 P.M.

  4. Quentin was a great musician he always drew large crowds.

B If a sentence is correct, write *C*. If it has mistakes in punctuation, rewrite it, adding the needed marks.

1. Mr. Casey hates country western music to him, it is simply noise.

2. I'd like to convince him that this music—I've loved it since I was very young—is worthwhile.

3. An ad in the Salem Chronicle said several well known performers would be playing in concert.

4. I invited Mr. Casey to attend; I didn't mention the performers.

5. The concert would start at 800 P.M. sharp we set out at about 630.

6. Twenty five minutes after we arrived, Mr. Casey—I never saw his face so red before was ready to leave.

C Write a letter that contains each of the following groups of words. Add today's date and an appropriate closing. Use colons, hyphens, semicolons, dashes, and underlining in your letter.

Dear Sir or Madam
thirty five good seats
her best selling book Flying to the Moon
either the 100 or the 300 show
something we've been looking forward to since last year
some students will come by bus some will walk
an article in the Miami Herald
tickets for us at the main floor box office

Test Preparation

Write the letter of the choice that correctly completes each sentence.

1. Music class is ____ on Tuesdays.

   A 1235 to 105
   B 12;35 to 1;05
   C 1235—105
   D 12:35 to 1:05

2. Our Music Club ordered ____ tickets.

   A twenty-five
   B twenty—five
   C twenty five
   D twenty:five

3. Sometimes I practice ____ I play with my friends.

   A alone—sometimes
   B alone; sometimes
   C alone: sometimes
   D alone-sometimes

4. The letter began, "Dear ____ Thank you."

   A Mr. Lewis-
   B Mr. Lewis;
   C Mr. Lewis:
   D Mr. Lewis

5. Ms. Ramirez is a ____ musician.

   A well known
   B well-known
   C well—known
   D wellknown

6. Dora plays the ____ also plays the flute.

   A piano: she
   B piano—she
   C piano; she
   D piano-she

7. Our textbook is ____.

   A Music for Everyone
   B Music-for-Everyone
   C Music—for Everyone
   D Music for Everyone

8. The competition ____ will include all city schools.

   A —it's been rescheduled three times—
   B ; it's been rescheduled three times;
   C it's been rescheduled three times
   D : it's been rescheduled three times:

Review

☑ Rewrite each sentence. Add the missing punctuation marks.

1. My piano lesson was changed from 400 P.M. to 300 P.M.

2. The book is called A Musical Surprise.

3. We looked at pictures of different instruments today I liked the tuba best.

4. Then we listened to instrument sounds this was fun and tried to match instruments to their sounds.

5. The flute has a high pitched, silvery sound.

6. A tuba's sound and looks are similar both are big, blustery, and funny.

7. My letter began, "Dear Mr. Colson I am interested in playing the tuba."

☑ Write *C* if a sentence is correct as written. If it has errors in punctuation, rewrite it correctly.

8. There was a good review of yesterday's performance in the <u>Springfield Gazette</u>.

9. I'll meet you at 80:0 A.M. I know that's early at the bus stop.

10. My solo lasts exactly forty two seconds it seems like an hour or two!

11. Dear Mr. Quinn

   Please reserve the concert hall from 300: P.M. to 500: P.M. on Tuesday, May 3.

12. I'd love to be a rock star unfortunately, I have no talent.

13. Though critics said she would never succeed, she has recorded twenty-seven hits so far.

14. Her friends I am one of them always knew she would be successful.

Topic Sentence

All the sentences in a paragraph should tell about one main idea. Often the main idea is stated in a **topic sentence**. This sentence may appear anywhere in the paragraph, but often it is the first sentence.

 Write the letter of the topic sentence that goes with each group of details.

Topic Sentences

A For the first time, African American artists were acknowledged by the public.

B Harlem artists expressed their roots and longings through their works.

1. • told stories of their history in Africa and the South

• expressed their racial pride

• talked about their desire for equality

2. • everyone excited by jazz inventions

• African American writers praised by critics

• novels, stories, poems, plays published

 Write a topic sentence based on the following details.

improvisation—music made up on the spot

• an important part of jazz

• musician creates during performance

• makes jazz exciting and fresh

• listeners often respond with surprise and delight

Informational Article

An **informational article** gives readers facts about a topic. The writer may be an expert on the subject or a student like you who has researched the subject. An effective informational article presents facts in a way that is easy for the nonexpert reader to understand. The model below is part of an informational article.

Jazz in Harlem

Introduction tells topic of article. ——

In the 1920s, the New York neighborhood of Harlem was a birthplace for great African American art and music. Many African American artists and musicians lived and worked there at that time. The special music of Harlem was jazz.

Topic sentence tells main idea of paragraph. ——

Detail sentences support main idea. ——

Jazz began in the African American community, where music accompanied work, play, marriages, births, and deaths. Jazz came from slave work songs, blues, gospel, and Creole music in the South. By the 1920s, it had become popular in Harlem and throughout America.

Where could you go in Harlem to hear jazz musicians? The Apollo Theater, the Cotton Club, and the Savoy Ballroom were all popular places. In them, you could hear Duke Ellington, Cab Calloway, and Ella Fitzgerald.

Taking Tests

Follow these tips when writing for a test:

Before Writing

- Read the prompt carefully. What does it ask you to do?
- Write down key words that name your audience (warn <u>people who eat junk food</u>), state the purpose of the composition (<u>give directions</u>), and tell you how to organize your points (provide <u>step-by-step instructions</u>).
- Use a graphic organizer to plan your composition.
- Determine the tone of your writing (friendly, formal).

During Writing

- Reread the prompt as you write to make sure you are on topic.
- Keep in mind your graphic organizer and stay focused.
- Write a good beginning. You might engage readers with a thought-provoking question or an interesting fact.
- Develop and elaborate ideas. Support your main idea, your observations, or your opinion.
- Write a strong ending. Try to write a "clincher" sentence to provide a clear ending. You might add a final comment of your own or challenge your reader with a command.

After Writing

- Check your grammar and mechanics (punctuation, spelling).
- Reread the prompt and review your work. There's still time to add words or correct errors.

Writing a Personal Narrative

A **test** may ask you to write a personal narrative. Your narrative should have a beginning, middle, and end. Use clue words such as *once* and *now* to show the order of events. Follow the tips below.

Understand the prompt.   Read the prompt carefully. A prompt for a personal narrative could look like this:

Think about an exciting experience or memorable event in your life. Write a personal narrative about it.

Key words and phrases are *experience, event in your life,* and *personal narrative.*

Find a good topic.   Visualize important events in your life and make a list. Choose an event that has interesting or exciting details.

Organize your ideas.   Write a time line on scratch paper to help organize the order of events.

Mom got a job.	We moved to Texas.	I went to a new school and felt lost!	I made a friend.	Now I have many friends.
Date or Time				
June	August	September 1	September 4	Today

Write a good beginning.   A good introductory sentence will grab your reader's attention.

Develop and elaborate ideas.   Use your time line to help organize events. Include vivid words and a variety of sentences. Use complete sentences.

Write a strong ending. Consider ending your personal narrative by describing how you felt about the events that took place.

Check your work. Decide if anything needs to be changed.

See how the personal narrative below addresses the prompt.

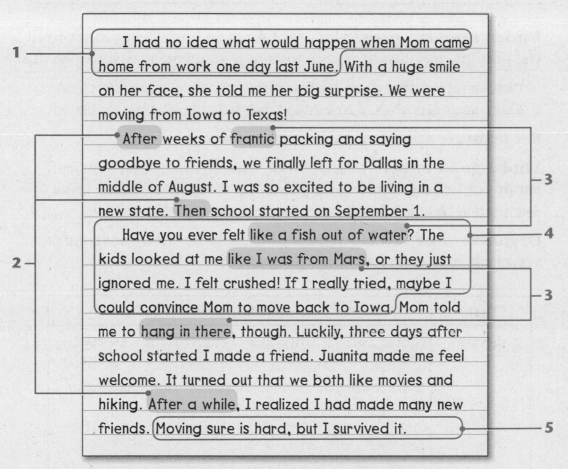

1 — I had no idea what would happen when Mom came home from work one day last June. With a huge smile on her face, she told me her big surprise. We were moving from Iowa to Texas!

After weeks of frantic packing and saying goodbye to friends, we finally left for Dallas in the middle of August. I was so excited to be living in a new state. Then school started on September 1. — 3

Have you ever felt like a fish out of water? The kids looked at me like I was from Mars, or they just ignored me. I felt crushed! If I really tried, maybe I could convince Mom to move back to Iowa. Mom told me to hang in there, though. Luckily, three days after school started I made a friend. Juanita made me feel welcome. It turned out that we both like movies and hiking. After a while, I realized I had made many new friends. Moving sure is hard, but I survived it. — 5

— 4

— 3

2

1. The opening sentence gets the reader's attention.

2. Transitions show the order of events.

3. Vivid words and phrases establish the writer's voice.

4. A variety of sentences makes writing flow smoothly.

5. This strong ending clearly shows the writer's feelings.

Writing a How-to Report

A **test** may ask you to write a how-to report. Be sure to include all the steps. Remember to use time-order words such as *first, next,* and *last* to show the order of steps. Follow the tips below.

Understand the prompt. Make sure you know what to do. Read the prompt carefully. A prompt for a how-to report may look like this:

> Write a report that gives steps on how to make or do something. Make your report easy to understand. Include materials needed.

Key terms are *report, steps, how to make or do,* and *materials.*

Find a good topic. Make a list of possible topics. Narrow your list by considering these questions: *What are the basic steps? What information should I include? Can I present the steps clearly?*

Organize your ideas. Write a how-to chart. Write the name of your task, materials, and a list of steps.

Task	Making paper
Steps	Gather materials (newspapers torn in strips, blender, white glue, sink, water, coat hanger, old pantyhose).
	Make frames out of coat hanger wire and pantyhose.
	Put paper and water in blender. Blend 2 minutes.
	Put water, glue, and paper pulp in sink. Mix well.
	Scoop pulp onto frame and lift slowly.
	Drain, dry, and peel off.

Write a good beginning.   Write a catchy opening sentence.

Develop and elaborate ideas.   Organize the steps.

Write a strong ending.   Write a clear, strong conclusion.

Check your work.   Is any information missing?

See how the report below addresses the prompt.

1 — Make your old, used paper live again! Create your own sheets of paper while you recycle. You will need

2 — newspapers torn in strips, a blender, white glue, a sink, water, coat hangers, and old pantyhose.

First, straighten a coat hanger and shape it into a square. Tape the ends together and carefully stretch a leg of pantyhose over the frame. Now fill the blender one-third full with paper strips and add water up to the two-thirds mark. Blend on high for 2 minutes. — 4

3 — Next, put the pulp, two teaspoons of glue, and several inches of water in the sink. Mix everything together well. Then slide a frame in under the water, level it, and wiggle it until it is covered with an even layer of pulp. Slowly lift the frame out of the water and let it drain for a minute. Put the frame in the sun to dry.

Peel off the paper and feel good about saving a tree! — 5

1. The first sentence captures attention.

2. The introduction tells the purpose and lists materials.

3. Time-order words show order of steps.

4. Directions give specific measurements.

5. A strong ending sums up and reminds about recycling.

Writing a Compare/Contrast Essay

A **test** may ask you to write a compare/contrast essay. Choose subjects that are alike and different. Follow the tips below.

Understand the prompt. Make sure you know what to do. Read the prompt carefully. A prompt could look like this:

Compare and contrast two important inventions and the effect they have had on people's lives. Include important similarities and differences between the inventions.

Key words are *compare, contrast, inventions, effect, similarities,* and *differences*.

Find a good topic. Think of inventions that you believe are really important. Then choose two that are both similar and different.

Organize your ideas. Fill in a chart like the one below.

How are the inventions alike?	Car and airplane both are transportation. Both have motors and wheels.
How are they different?	Airplane much faster, used by fewer people. Cars used by everybody, good for close or far destinations.

Write a good beginning. Write a strong topic sentence.

Develop and elaborate ideas. Use your chart to organize ideas.

Write a strong ending. Use the ending to sum up your ideas.

Check your work. Have you used words to indicate likenesses and differences?

See how the essay below addresses the prompt.

1 — The automobile and the airplane are both important inventions that changed life for people. Both inventions are forms of transportation that use engines and wheels. Both also greatly improved the speed and quality of travel for people. In addition, both helped bring distant areas closer.

However, there are many differences between these inventions. For example, airplanes travel much faster than automobiles. They are used by fewer people than cars because it is expensive to buy a ticket. Also, people living far from an airport may not always find planes convenient. On the other hand, cars are everywhere because many people can afford them. Cars can be used to travel to most destinations, but planes aren't economical for a short trip. Cars and airplanes fill different needs, but both are necessary in our fast-moving world.

1. The first sentence explains what will be compared.
2. The writer organizes similarities, then differences.
3. The writer uses signal words throughout the essay.
4. The strong ending sums up the essay.

Writing a Story

A **test** may ask you to write a story. Think of a problem and characters you could write about, and tell a story about how the characters solve the problem. Follow the tips below.

Understand the prompt.   Make sure you know what to do. Read the prompt carefully. A prompt for a story could look like this:

> Write a story about a person and an animal. Tell about how they learn to get along with each other. Be sure your story has a beginning, middle, and end.

Key words are *story, person, animal, get along, beginning, middle,* and *end.*

Find a good topic.   Imagine characters that appeal to you and a story in which they can learn to get along.

Organize your ideas.   Fill in a story chart like the one below.

Story about how a boy befriends a wild dog	
Characters Umesh and a young wild dog	
Setting the woods behind Umesh's house	
Action	
Beginning Umesh sees a starving dog in woods. It runs away. He decides to feed it. **Middle** He brings food every day. Slowly, he can move closer while dog eats. **End** Finally, he can touch the dog. They become friends.	

Write a good beginning.   Introduce the characters, setting, and problem in your beginning.

Develop and elaborate ideas. Use your chart to organize events. Include vivid, specific words to bring events to life. Use dialogue.

Write a strong ending. Show how the problem was resolved.

Check your work. Decide if anything needs to be changed.

See how the story below addresses the prompt.

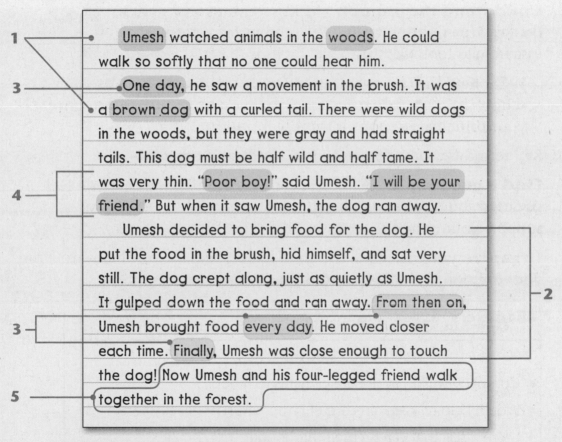

1.   Umesh watched animals in the woods. He could walk so softly that no one could hear him.

3.   One day, he saw a movement in the brush. It was a brown dog with a curled tail. There were wild dogs in the woods, but they were gray and had straight tails. This dog must be half wild and half tame. It was very thin. "Poor boy!" said Umesh. "I will be your

4.   friend." But when it saw Umesh, the dog ran away.

  Umesh decided to bring food for the dog. He put the food in the brush, hid himself, and sat very still. The dog crept along, just as quietly as Umesh. It gulped down the food and ran away. From then on,

2.

3.   Umesh brought food every day. He moved closer each time. Finally, Umesh was close enough to touch the dog! Now Umesh and his four-legged friend walk

5.   together in the forest.

1. The writer quickly introduces characters and setting.
2. Umesh's actions reveal his character.
3. The writer reports events in clear time order.
4. The writer shows the characters' feelings.
5. The ending tells how the problem was resolved.

Writing a Persuasive Essay

A **test** may ask you to write a persuasive essay. Support your opinion with examples, facts, reasons, and words and phrases such as *should* and *most important*. Follow the tips below.

Understand the prompt.   Make sure you know what to do. Read the prompt carefully. A prompt for a persuasive essay could look like this:

> What new club or organization would you like to have at your school? Write a persuasive essay that you might use to convince your principal to sponsor this organization.

Key terms are *club* or *organization, school,* and *convince.*

Find a good topic.   Choose a club or organization that you feel strongly about. Be sure you can think of enough good reasons to support your opinion.

Organize your ideas.   Use an organizer like the one below to write your opinion and to list reasons that support your opinion.

Opinion: Our school should sponsor a photography club.

Reasons

- Company willing to donate cameras to school.
- Would help us keep a record of important school activities.
- Learn a skill that can be used throughout life.
- Everybody should know how to use a camera.
- Hobby that can be done anywhere.

Write a good beginning.   Write an opening sentence that grabs the reader's attention and clearly states your opinion.

Develop and elaborate ideas. Use the organizer to focus your writing. Use powerful words and convincing reasons.

Write a strong ending. Let the ending sum up your opinion. Save your strongest reason for the end.

Check your work. Have you supported your opinion?

See how the persuasive argument below addresses the prompt.

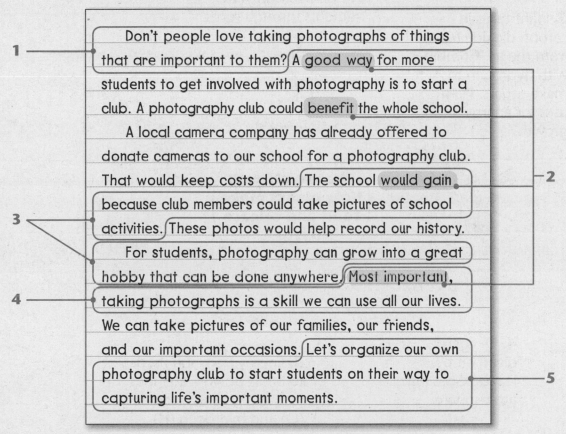

1   Don't people love taking photographs of things that are important to them? A good way for more students to get involved with photography is to start a club. A photography club could benefit the whole school.

    A local camera company has already offered to donate cameras to our school for a photography club. That would keep costs down. The school would gain   2
3   because club members could take pictures of school activities. These photos would help record our history.

    For students, photography can grow into a great hobby that can be done anywhere. Most important,
4   taking photographs is a skill we can use all our lives. We can take pictures of our families, our friends, and our important occasions. Let's organize our own photography club to start students on their way to   5
capturing life's important moments.

1. An opening question attracts readers' attention.
2. The writer uses persuasive words effectively.
3. Complex sentences present reasons, causes, and effects.
4. The argument builds to the most important reason.
5. A strong ending sums up the writer's thoughts.

Writing a Summary

Some **tests** may ask you to summarize information from a time line, diagram, or chart. You will need to read the information carefully and use it to develop your own sentences.

1. Plants take in water, nutrients through roots.

5. Plant takes in carbon dioxide (CO2) from the air. Combines with hydrogen to make sugars. Plant uses for energy and growth.

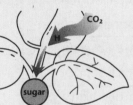

CO₂

H

sugar

Photosynthesis: How plants make food and release oxygen

2. Plant cells absorb sunlight.

O₂

O₂

O₂

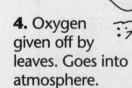

O

H

H

4. Oxygen given off by leaves. Goes into atmosphere.

3. Energy from sun used to break down water into its two elements, oxygen (O) and hydrogen (H).

Organize your ideas. In a diagram like this one, you will need to locate the starting point. Be sure to put words into complete sentences and provide a beginning and a conclusion.

Write a good beginning. Think of a topic sentence that states the main idea you want to present about your subject.

Develop and elaborate ideas. Include all important details from the diagram. Tell how the details support your main idea.

Write a strong ending. Tie information together effectively.

Check your work. Is your summary accurate?

See how the summary below is based on the diagram.

1 —
2 —

    Plants do not eat like people do. Instead, a green plant produces its own food, using a process called photosynthesis. The process begins as water and nutrients come into the plant. They enter through the roots and travel upward. Sunlight strikes the leaves of the plant, and the plant absorbs some of the energy from the sunlight. The water and the sunlight provide the plant with the raw materials it needs to begin photosynthesis.

    The plant cells use the energy from sunlight to break water down into oxygen and hydrogen. Then the oxygen atoms are given off by the leaves and go into the atmosphere. At the same time, carbon dioxide from the air enters the leaves. It combines with the hydrogen to form sugar. Through this chain of events, the plant has made food, which it will use for energy and growing.

3 —
— 4
— 5

1. These sentences draw interest and state an important fact.
2. These sentences define a key term.
3. Details all point to the main idea.
4. The writer shows connections between steps.
5. The ending ties the information together.

Grammar Patrol

Grammar Patrol

adjective   An adjective describes a noun or a pronoun.

Ponds are *active* places.
Several chipmunks run through the *wet* grass.

Adjectives have two different forms that are used to make comparisons.

- Use the *–er* form of an adjective to compare two persons, places, or things.

   Frogs have *smoother* skin than toads.

- Use the *–est* form of an adjective to compare three or more persons, places, or things.

   Snails are the *slowest* pond creatures.

- The words *more* and *most* are often used with adjectives of two or more syllables to make comparisons.

   The ducks were *more comical* than usual.
   The goose is the *most common* bird here.

- Some adjectives show comparison in a special way. The correct forms of *good*, *bad*, *much*, and *little* are shown below.

good weather	*better* weather	*best* weather
bad storm	*worse* storm	*worst* storm
much snow	*more* snow	*most* snow
little fog	*less* fog	*least* fog

article   The words, *a*, *an*, and *the* are a special kind of adjective. They are called articles. *The* is used with both singular and plural nouns. *A* and *an* are used only with singular nouns.

The animals at *the* pond are very busy.
A friend and I spent *an* afternoon there.

- Use *a* before a word that begins with a consonant sound.

   a beaver   *a* pleasant afternoon

- Use *an* before a word that begins with a vowel sound.

   an owl   *an* underwater plant

adverb   A word that describes a verb is an adverb.

- Some adverbs ask the question "How?"

    The fox hides *slyly* behind the bushes. (how?)

- Some adverbs answer the question "Where?"

    Aesop wrote fables *here*. (where?)

- Other adverbs answer the question "When?"

    Often a fable tells about one event. (when?)

Adverbs can be used to compare actions.

- Use the *–er* form or *more* to compare two actions. Most adverbs that end in *–ly* use *more*.

    The ant worked *harder* than the cricket.
    The tortoise moved *more steadily* than the hare.

- Use the *–est* form or *most* to compare three or more actions. Most adverbs that end in *–ly* use *most*.

    The ant worked *hardest* of all the insects.
    The tortoise moved *most steadily* of all.

The word *not* is an adverb. It means "no." Do not use two words that mean "no" in the same sentence.

    Wrong: It *wouldn't never* matter to me.
    Right: It *wouldn't* ever matter to me.
    Right: It would *never* matter to me.

contraction   A contraction is a shortened form of two words. An apostrophe replaces a letter or letters.

- Some contractions join a pronoun and a verb.

    I have never been in a dairy shed before.
    I've never been in a dairy shed before.

- Some contractions are formed from a verb and the word *not*.

    I *cannot* believe you *did not* bring your banjo.
    I *can't* believe you *didn't* bring your banjo.

noun   A noun names a person, place, or thing.

The *settlers* came to *America* on a *ship*.

(person)   (place)   (thing)

A **singular noun** names one person, place, or thing.

The *settler* kept the *cow* in the *barn*.

A **plural noun** names more than one person, place, or thing.

The *settlers* kept their *cows* in their *barns*.

- Add *-s* to form the plural of most nouns.

  colonist*s*   river*s*   pea*s*   chicken*s*

- Add *-es* to form the plural of nouns that end in *ch*, *sh*, *s*, *ss*, *x*, or *z*.

  bench*es*   bush*es*   bus*es*   box*es*

- If a noun ends in a consonant and *y*, change *y* to *i* and add *-es* to form the plural.

  Singular: library   city   cherry
  Plural: librar*ies*   cit*ies*   cherr*ies*

- Some plurals are formed by changing the spelling of the singular noun.

  Singular: man   child   foot   mouse
  Plural: men   child*ren*   feet   mice

- A few nouns have the same singular and plural forms.

  Singular: elk   moose   deer   sheep
  Plural: elk   moose   deer   sheep

A **common noun** names any person, place, or thing.

A *colonist* founded the *town*.

A **proper noun** names a particular person, place, or thing.

William Penn founded *Philadelphia*.

A **possessive noun** shows ownership.

- To form the possessive of a singular noun, add an apostrophe and *s* (*'s*) to the singular noun.

    Ben Franklin's many talents amazed people.

- To form the possessive of a plural noun ending in *s*, add an apostrophe (*s'*).

    shoemakers' hammers   *blacksmiths'* forges

- To form the possessive of a plural noun that does not end in *s*, add an apostrophe and *s* (*'s*).

    men's hats   *mice's* tails   two *deer's* tracks

preposition   A preposition is a word that shows how a noun or pronoun is related to other words in the same sentence.

    We sing *in* the car.

A preposition begins a group of words called a **prepositional phrase**. At the end of the phrase is a noun or pronoun called the **object of the preposition**.

    Preposition: The dog buried its bone *in* the yard.
    Prepositional phrase: *in the yard*
    Object of the proposition: *yard*

pronoun   A pronoun takes the place of a noun or nouns.

    Nouns: *Linda* writes *poems*.
    Pronouns: *She* enjoys writing *them*.

The pronouns *I, you, she, he, it, we,* and *they* are **subject pronouns**. Use these pronouns to replace nouns that are the subjects of sentences.

    Robert Frost had been a teacher and a farmer.
    He wrote many poems about nature.

The pronouns *me, you, him, her, it, us* and *them* are **object pronouns**. You can use these pronouns to replace nouns in the predicate of a sentence.

> Paul read *poems* to *Jill*.
> Paul read *them* to *her*.

The pronouns *my, your, his, her, its, our,* and *their* are **possessive pronouns**. A possessive pronoun shows ownership. Possessive pronouns can replace nouns.

> That *writer's* home is in the mountains.
> *Her* poems usually involve nature.

sentence   A sentence is a group of words that expresses a complete thought.

> *People of all ages enjoy hobbies.*

A **declarative sentence** makes a statement. It ends with a period (.).

> *Hobbies are important in people's lives.*

An **interrogative sentence** asks a question. It ends with a question mark (?).

> *What is your hobby?*

An **imperative sentence** gives a command or makes a request. It usually ends with a period (.).

> *Please get your kite ready. Come to our party!*

An **exclamatory sentence** expresses strong feeling. It ends with an exclamation mark (!).

> *That kite will crash!*   *How happy I am!*

A **simple sentence** has one subject and one predicate. It expresses one complete thought.

> *Kites come in many different shapes.*

A **compound sentence** contains two simple sentences joined by the word *and*, *but*, or *or*. Use a comma in a compound sentence before the word *and*, *but*, or *or*.

>*The day was cool*, and *clouds drifted across the sun.*

subject and predicate The subject is the part of the sentence that names someone or something. The predicate tells what the subject is or does. Both the subject and the predicate may be one word or many words.

>*Currents/move ocean water around the world.*
>*The most common mineral/is salt.*
>*Ocean water/moves.*
>*Sea water/flows in vast streams.*

The **simple subject** is the main word in the complete subject.

>The five biggest *oceans* are really one huge ocean.

A sentence may have more than one simple subject. The word *and* may be used to join simple subjects, making a **compound subject**. The simple subjects share the same predicate.

>Spiny *crabs* and colorful *fish* scurry along the underwater reef.

The **simple predicate** is the main word or words in the complete predicate.

>Ocean waters *flow* in vast streams.

A sentence may have more than one simple predicate. The word *and* may be used to join simple predicates, making a **compound predicate**. The simple predicates share the same subject.

>Some worms *live* and *feed* in the ocean.

verb A verb is a word that shows action or being.

>Nina *paints* in art class. (action)
>That picture *is* beautiful. (being)

An **action verb** shows action. It tells what the subject of a sentence does.

> The art teacher *welcomed* the students.

A verb can be more than one word. The **main verb** is the most important verb. A **helping verb** works with the main verb.

> Many people have *admired* Picasso's paintings. (main verb)
> His name *is* known all over the world. (helping verb)

A **linking verb** shows being. It tells what the subject is or was.

> Grandma Moses *was* a famous artist.

When the correct subject and verb are used together, we say they agree. The form of the linking verb *be* that is used depends on the subject of the sentence. Study the following chart.

Using the Forms of *be*

Use *am* and *was*	with *I*
Use *is* and *was*	with *she, he, it,* and singular nouns
Use *are* and *were*	with *we, you, they,* and plural nouns

The **tense** of a verb shows the time of the action.

A verb in the **present tense** shows action that happens now.

> Eli *forms* the tiles.

A verb in the present tense must agree with the subject of the sentence.

- With *he, she, it,* or a singular noun, add *-s* or *-es* to the verb.

> The student learn*s*.   My cousin teach*es*.   He walk*s*.

- If a verb ends in *ch, sh, s, ss, x,* or *z,* add *-es*. Notice the word *teaches* above.

- With *I, you, we, they,* or a plural noun, do not add *-s* or *-es*.

> The students learn.   My cousins teach.   They walk.

A verb in the **future tense** shows action that will happen. The future tense is formed with the helping verb *will*.

> Ann *will create* a vase.

A verb in the **past tense** shows action that already happened.

Lee *washed* pots.

The past tenses of irregular verbs are not formed by adding *-ed*. Some irregular verbs are shown in the following chart.

Verb	Past	Past with *have*, *has*, or *had*
begin	began	begun
bring	brought	brought
come	came	come
do	did	done
eat	ate	eaten
fall	fell	fallen
find	found	found
fly	flew	flown
give	gave	given
go	went	gone
grow	grew	grown
ride	rode	ridden
run	ran	run
see	saw	seen
take	took	taken
throw	threw	thrown
write	wrote	written

The spelling of some verbs changes when *-es* or *-ed* is added.

- If a verb ends in a consonant and *y*, change the *y* to *i* before adding *-es* or *-ed*.

  study   stud*ies*   stud*ied*

- If a verb ends in one vowel and one consonant, double the final consonant before adding *-ed*.

  trap   tra*pped*   stir   sti*rred*

Capitalization

first word of a sentence   Every sentence begins with a capital letter.

People enjoy having special projects.

proper noun   Each important word in a proper noun begins with a capital letter.

- Capitalize each word in the name of a person or pet.

   Patrice Gomez owns a cat named *Duke.*

- Capitalize an initial in a name. Put a period after the initial.

   William *L.* Chen is a doctor in our neighborhood.

- Capitalize a title before a name. If the title is an *abbreviation* (a shortened form of a word), put a period after it.

   President Jefferson   *Dr.* Jonas Salk

- Capitalize every important word in the names of particular places or things.

   Statue of Liberty   *Ellis Island*   *New York Harbor*

- Capitalize names of days, months, holidays, and special days.

   Tuesday   *April*   *Fourth of July*

pronoun *I*   The pronoun *I* is always capitalized.

May *I* go skating this afternoon?

letter   Capitalize the first word of the greeting and the first word of the closing of a letter.

Dear Mother,   *Dear* Sir: *Sincerely* yours,

title of books, movies, songs, and other works   Capitalize the first word, the last word, and all of the important words in the title of works.

The Secret Life of Harold the Bird Watcher
"The Star-Spangled Banner"

quotation Begin the first word in a quotation with a capital letter.

> The Hare asked, *"How* about a race?"

Punctuation

period Declarative sentences and imperative sentences end with a period (.).

> *I stood on the corner.*   *Wait for the signal.*

- Put a period after an initial in a name.

> J. P. Jones   Abigail S. Adams

- Put a period after an abbreviation (a shortened form of a word).

> *Mr.*   *Mrs.*   *Ms.*   *Dr.*

question mark An interrogative sentence ends with a question mark (?).

> *Do you have more than one hobby?*

exclamation mark An exclamatory sentence ends with an exclamation mark (!).

> *That kite will crash!*

comma A comma (,) is a signal that tells a reader to pause.

- Use a comma after *yes, no,* or *well* at the beginning of a sentence.

> *Yes,* I saw the display of Eskimo art.
> *Well,* my favorites were the bears made of silver.

- Use a comma to set off the name of the person spoken to.

> *Your painting is very beautiful, Roberta.*

- Use a comma to separate words in a series. A series is made up of three or more items. No comma is used after the last word in the series. The last comma goes before the word *and.*

> *The artists carve, smooth, and polish their work.*

- Use a comma to separate the city from the state.

    I grew up in *Tulsa, Oklahoma.*

- Use a comma to separate the day and the year.

    Pablo was born on *February 7, 2000.*

- Use a comma after the greeting of a friendly letter. Use a comma after the closing of a friendly or a business letter.

    Dear Kim,   *Your friend,*   *Yours truly,*

- Use a comma before the word *and*, *but*, or *or* in a compound sentence.

    The merchants crossed central Asia, and they reached China.

quotation marks   A quotation is the exact words someone speaks. Quotation marks (" ") show where a speaker's exact words begin and end.

- Use quotation marks before and after a quotation. Begin the first word in a quotation with a capital letter. When the quotation comes last, use a comma to separate the speaker from the quotation.

    The Tortoise said, "I'm not going to lose this race."

- When the quotation comes first, use a comma, a question mark, or an exclamation mark to separate the quotation from the speaker. The end mark of a quotation always comes just before the second quotation mark. Put a period at the end of the sentence.

    Statement: "Let's do something else," replied the Tortoise.
    Question: "Are you afraid you'll lose?" teased the Hare.
    Exclamation: "I'm not afraid!" snapped the Tortoise.

- Enclose the titles of stories, songs, poems, and articles in quotation marks.

    Story: "The Use of Force"
    Song: "Of Thee I Sing"
    Poem: "Dear March, Come In!"
    Article: "Let's Make Music"

Underline the titles of newspapers, magazines, books, plays, and movies.

In materials you read, these titles are printed in italics.

Newspaper: <u>Denver Post</u>
Magazine: <u>Popular Mechanics</u>
Book: <u>A Wind in the Door</u>
Play: <u>Man of La Mancha</u>
Movie: <u>Invaders from Mars</u>

apostrophe   Use an apostrophe (') to show where a letter or letters have been left out in a *contraction* (a shortened form of two words).

we'd (we + had)   *wasn't* (was + not)

• Use an apostrophe to form the possessive of a noun.

man's   *James's*   *men's*   *workers'*

colon   Use a colon (:) after the greeting in a business letter.

Dear Mr. Kurtz: *Dear Sir or Madam:*

Frequently Misspelled Words

a lot
afraid
again
almost
already
always
another
are
athlete
basketball
beautiful
because
before
believe
brother
brought
buy
caught
chocolate
Christmas
clothes
control
could
cousin
Dad's
decided
didn't
different
disappear
doesn't
don't
enough
especially
everybody
everyone

everything
except
excited
family
favorite
February
field
finally
first
found
friend
getting
government
grabbed
happened
heard
hero
his
hospital
house
I
I'm
instead
into
it's
knew
know
knowledge
let's
library
little
maybe
might
minute
Mom

morning
myself
of
off
once
one
opened
our
outside
people
piece
presents
pretty
probably
radio
really
right
said
scared
school
separate
should
since
sincerely
something
sometimes
special
started
stopped
successful
sure
surprised
swimming
that's
their

then
there
they
they're
thought
through
to
too
took
tries
truly
TV
two
until
upon
usually
vacation
very
want
was
watch
weird
went
we're
were
what
when
where
which
who
whole
with
would
you're

D'Nealian™ Alphabet

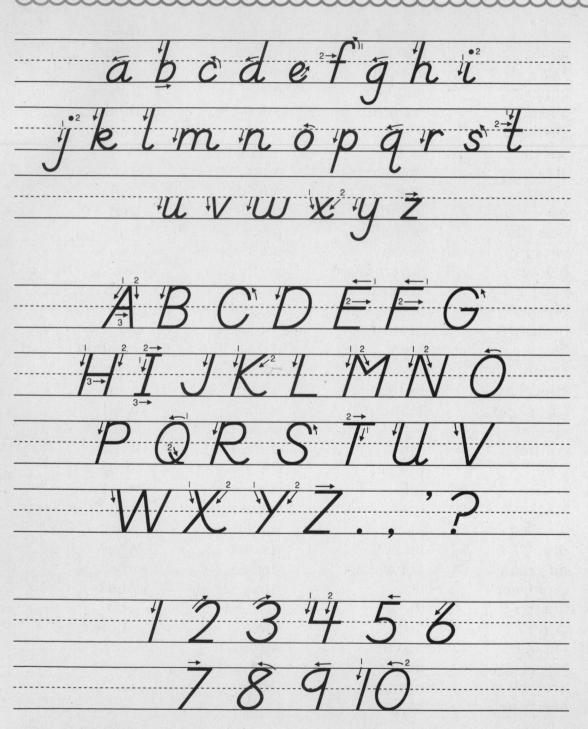

Manuscript Alphabet

Cursive Alphabet

a b c d e f g
h i j k l m m n
o p q r s t u
v w x y z

A B C D E F G
H I J K L M N
O P Q R S T U
V W X Y Z . , ' ?

1 2 3 4 5 6
7 8 9 10

Index

Index

D

Dash, 224–227
Declarative sentences. *See* Sentences.
Dependent clauses. *See* Clauses.
Descriptive writing. *See* Writing.
Details, 2–3, 168
Direct address. *See* Commas.

E

Evaluate your writing, 46–48
Exclamation mark, 50–53
Expository writing. *See* Writing.
Exclamatory sentences. *See* Sentences.

F

Focus/Ideas. *See* Writing.
Fragments, 56–59
Frequently misspelled words, 257

H

Handwriting, 258–260
Helping verbs. *See* Verbs.
Hyperbole, 217
Hyphen, 224–227

I

Imperative sentences. *See* Sentences.

Indefinite pronouns. *See* Pronouns.
Independent clauses. *See* Clauses.
Interjections, 50–53
Interrogative sentences. *See* Sentences.
Introductory words and phrases. *See* Commas.
Irregular verbs. *See* Verbs.
Italics, 224–227
Items in series. *See* Commas.

L

Linking verbs. *See* Verbs.

M

Main idea, 2–3
Main verb. *See* Verbs.
Mechanics, 254–256
   apostrophe, 86–89, 170–173
   colon, 224–227
   comma, 62–65, 68–71, 206–209, 218–221
   dash, 224–227
   exclamation mark, 50–53, 218–221
   hyphen, 224–227
   italics, 224–227
   period, 50–53, 74–77
   question mark, 50–53, 218–221

Index

Index